THE

HANDRAIL

THE HANDRAIL PUBLISHING COMPANY
1016 ARTHUR COURT, BOX 331
SALISBURY, MARYLAND 21804

PUBLISHING HISTORY

First Edition

Promotional Printing (42 copies)   JANUARY, 2007

UNITED STATES OF AMERICA
LIBRARY OF CONGRESS COPYRIGHT NUMBER: TX 6-221-202   2005

I.S.B.N. - 13: 978-0-9792169-0-9
I.S.B.N. - 10: 0-9792169-0-7   .

Published in the United States of America

i

TO THOSE IN THE FELLOWSHIPS OF RECOVERY
FROM ALCOHOL AND /OR NARCOTICS ADDICTION:
YOUNG AND OLD;
MEN AND WOMEN;
NEWCOMERS AND OLDTIMERS.

AS WITH MOST SETS OF STEPS, THERE WILL BE A HANDRAIL TO
HOLD ON TO AS WE MOVE FROM ONE STEP TO ANOTHER. THIS
HANDRAIL HELPS TO PREVENT US FROM FALLING AND POSSIBLITY
HURTING OURSELVES SERIOUSLY.   AND SO IT IS, ALSO, WITH THE
TWELVE STEPS OF RECOVERY. OUR "HANDRAIL" IS THE MANY
STORIES, THOUGHTS, AND SLOGANS THAT WE HEAR IN THE ROOMS
OF RECOVERY.

FOR HELP IN THE COLLECTION OF THIS MATERIAL, I AM TRULY
GRATEFUL TO MY FRIEND AND SPONSOR, JIM L., THE MEN AND
WOMEN WHO LIVE AND CARRY THE MESSAGE OF RECOVERY, AND
TO THE HOME GROUPS OF RECOVERY FOR THEIR EXISTENCE. I AM
ESPECIALLY GREATFUL TO THE DAMASCUS HOUSE, OF BROOKLYN,
MARYLAND, (THE CADILLAC OF ALL HALF-WAY HOUSES ON THE
ENTIRE EAST COAST OF AMERICA) FOR GRANTING ME PERMISSION
TO USE A PHOTOGRAPH OF THE ENTERANCE TO MY HOME GROUP'S
OLD MEETING PLACE ON THE COVER OF THIS BOOK.

IN THE SPIRIT OF "PASSING IT ON," A PORTION OF THE NET
PROCEEDS OF THIS PUBLICATION WILL GO TOWARDS THE
PURCHASE OF RECOVERY LITERATURE, IN PAPERBACK FORM,
WHICH WILL BE DONATED TO THOSE THAT ARE INSTITUTIONAL-
IZED OR INCARCERATED AS A RESULT OF THEIR ADDICTION.

1. EASY DOES IT.

2. FIRST THINGS FIRST.

3. LIVE AND LET LIVE.

4. BUT FOR THE GRACE OF GOD.

5. THINK...THINK...THINK.

6. ONE DAY AT A TIME.

7. LET GO AND LET GOD.

8. K.I.S.S.: KEEP IT SIMPLE SWEETHEART; KEEP IT SIMPLE STUPID.

9. IN LEARNING YOU WILL TEACH AND IN TEACHING YOU WILL LEARN.

10. THIS TOO SHALL PASS.

11. EXPECT MIRACLES.

12. I CAN'T... HE CAN... I'LL LET HIM.

13. IF IT WORKS...DON'T TRY TO FIX IT.

14. IT WORKS IF YOU LET IT.

15. STICK WITH THE WINNERS.

16. RECOVERY IS A JOURNEY...NOT A DESTINATION.

17. FAITH WITHOUT WORKS IS DEAD.

18. POOR ME...POOR ME...POUR ME ANOTHER DRINK.

19. TO THINE OWN SELF BE TRUE.

20. I CAME ... I CAME TO ... I CAME TO BELIEVE.

21. LIVE IN THE NOW.

22. IF GOD SEEMS FAR AWAY, THEN WHO MOVED?

23. TURN IT OVER.

24. N. A.: NEVER ALONE.

25. NOTHING IS SO BAD THAT PICKING UP AGAIN WON'T MAKE WORSE.

26. WE ARE ONLY AS SICK AS OUR SECRETS.

27. THERE ARE NO COINCIDENCES IN RECOVERY.

28. HOW CAN I DO RIGHT WITH A DO WRONG MIND?

29. IF YOU'RE NOT A PART OF THE SOLUTION, THEN YOU'RE A PART OF THE PROBLEM.

30. SPONSORS: HAVE ONE, USE ONE, BE ONE.

31. I CAN'T HANDLE IT GOD, YOU TAKE OVER.

32. KEEP AN OPEN MIND.

33. IT WORKS - - - IT REALLY DOES.

34. WILLINGNESS IS THE KEY.

35. RECOVERY ISN'T SIMPLY A MATTER OF NOT PICKING UP.

36. IF I DON'T USE WHAT I HAVE LEARNED, THEN I WILL LOSE WHAT I HAVE.

37. HIGHER POWERED.

38. NO PAIN...NO GAIN.

39. THERE IS A DIFFERENCE BETWEEN KNOWING THE PATH AND WALKING THE PATH.

40. PUT THE PLUG IN THE JUG AND THROW IT AWAY.

41. DO IT CLEAN AND SOBER.

42. LET IT BEGIN WITH ME.

43. JUST FOR TODAY.

44. SOBER N' CRAZY OR SOBER N' SERENE.

45. PASS IT ON.

46. IT'S IN THE BOOK.

47. YOU EITHER IS...OR YOU AIN'T.

48. BEFORE YOU SAY, "I CAN'T"...SAY, "I'LL TRY."

49. DON'T QUIT FIVE MINUTES BEFORE THE MIRACLE HAPPENS.

50. SOME ARE SICKER THAN OTHERS.

51. WE'RE ALL HERE BECAUSE WE'RE NOT ALL THERE.

52. ADDICTION IS AN EQUAL OPPORTUNITY DESTROYER.

53. PRACTICE AN ATTITUDE OF GRATITUDE.

54. THE ROAD TO RECOVERY IS SIMPLY A JOURNEY FOR CONFUSED PEOPLE WITH A COMPLICATED DISEASE.

55. ANOTHER FRIEND OF BILL W'S.

56. GOD IS NEVER LATE.

57. HAVE A GOOD DAY UNLESS OF COURSE YOU HAVE MADE OTHER PLANS.

58. DECISIONS AREN'T FOREVER.

59. IT TAKES TIME.

60. 90 MEETINGS IN 90 DAYS CAN BRING ABOUT A 180 IN YOUR LIFE.

61. YOU ARE NOT ALONE.

62. WHERE YOU GO...THERE YOU ARE.

63. DON'T PICK UP, READ YOUR "BASIC TEXT," AND GO TO MEETINGS.

64. USE THE TWENTY-FOUR HOUR PLAN.

65. MAKE USE OF THE TELEPHONE MEETINGS.

66. STAY CLEAN FOR YOURSELF.

67. LOOK FOR SIMILARITIES RATHER THAN DIFFERENCES.

68. REMEMBER YOUR LAST RUN.

69. REMEMBER THAT ADDICTION IS INCURABLE, PROGRESSIVE, AND FATAL.

70. TRY NOT TO PLACE CONDITIONS ON YOUR RECOVERY.

71. WHEN ALL ELSE FAILS, FOLLOW DIRECTIONS.

72. COUNT YOUR BLESSINGS.

73. RESPECT THE ANONYMITY OF OTHERS.

74. SHARE YOUR PAIN.

75. LET GO OF OLD IDEAS.

76. TRY TO REPLACE GUILT WITH GRATITUDE.

77. WHAT GOES AROUND COMES AROUND.

78. CHANGE IS A PROCESS, NOT AN EVENT.

79. TAKE THE COTTON OUT OF YOUR EARS AND PUT IT IN YOUR MOUTH.

80. CALL YOUR SPONSOR BEFORE YOU PICK UP, NOT AFTER.

81. SICK AND TIRED OF BEING SICK AND TIRED.

82. IT'S THE FIRST ONE THAT YOU PICK UP THAT TAKES YOU BACK OUT.

83. TO KEEP IT, YOU HAVE TO GIVE IT AWAY.

84. RECOVERY'S EXTREMITY IS GOD'S OPPORTUNITY.

85. THE PRICE OF SERENITY AND SANITY IS SELF-SACRIFICE.

86. ONE PERSON TALKING TO ANOTHER ... ONE EQUALS ONE.

87. TAKE WHAT YOU CAN USE AND LEAVE THE REST.

88. WHAT IF...

89. YEAH, BUT...

90. IF ONLY...

91. HELP IS ONLY A TELEPHONE CALL AWAY.

92. AROUND THE ROOMS OR IN THE ROOMS.

93. YOU CAN'T GIVE AWAY WHAT YOU DON'T HAVE.

94. ONE DRINK IS TOO MANY AND A THOUSAND IS NEVER ENOUGH.

95. KEEP COMING BACK.

96. ANGER IS BUT ONE LETTER AWAY FROM DANGER.

97. COURAGE TO CHANGE.

98. EASY DOES IT, BUT DO IT.

99. BRING THE BODY AND THE MIND WILL FOLLOW.

100. ACCEPT YOUR ADMISSION.

101. REMEMBER WHEN...

102. DRY UP AND TIGHTEN UP (FINANCIALLY).

103. WE, IN RECOVERY, ARE GIFTED PEOPLE.

104. THERE ARE TWELVE STEPS IN THE LADDER OF RECOVERY.

105. FEAR IS THE DARKROOM WHERE NEGATIVES ARE DEVELOPED.

106. BEFORE ENGAGING YOUR MOUTH, PUT YOUR MIND IN GEAR.

107. I WANT WHAT I WANT WHEN I WANT IT.

108. THERE IS NO CHEMICAL SOLUTION TO A SPIRITUAL PROBLEM.

109. RECOVERY IS NOT SOMETHING THAT YOU JOIN, IT'S A WAY OF LIFE.

110. WE CAN BE POSITIVE THAT OUR USING WAS NEGATIVE.

111. SPIRITUALITY IS THE ABILITY TO GET OUR MINDS OFF OURSELVES.

112. FAITH IS SPELLED A-C-T-I-O-N IN RECOVERY.

113. BACKSLIDING BEGINS WHEN KNEE-BENDING ENDS.

114. IF I THINK, I WON'T DRINK AND IF I DRINK, I WON'T THINK.

115. BEND YOUR KNEES BEFORE YOU BEND YOUR ELBOW.

116. THE FIRST STEP IN OVERCOMING MISTAKES IS TO ADMIT THEM.

117. FORMULA FOR FAILURE: TRY TO PLEASE EVERYONE.

118. SORROW IS LOOKING BACK AND WORRY IS LOOKING AROUND.

119. WILLPOWER: OUR WILL-INGNESS TO USE A HIGHER POWER.

120. RECOVERY IS AN EDUCATION WITHOUT A GRADUATION.

121. YOUR HEART STOPS GROWING WHEN YOUR HEAD BEGINS TO SWELL.

122. A JOURNEY OF A THOUSAND MILES BEGINS WITH THE FIRST STEP.

123. BE AS ENTHUSIASTIC ABOUT YOUR RECOVERY AS YOU WERE ABOUT YOUR PICKING UP.

124. HUMILITY IS OUR ACCEPTANCE OF OURSELVES.

125. TRYING TO PRAY IS PRAYING.

126. GET IT ... GIVE IT ... GROW IN IT.

127. FAITH IS NOT BELIEF WITHOUT PROOF, BUT TRUST WITHOUT RESERVATION.

128. WE'RE RESPONSIBLE FOR THE EFFORT, NOT THE OUTCOME.

129. THIS IS A SELFISH PROGRAM.

130. E.G.O.: EDGING GOD OUT.

131. KEEP YOUR RECOVERY FIRST TO MAKE IT LAST.

132. I DRANK TOO MUCH ... TOO OFTEN ... TOO LONG.

133. RECOVERY WILL WORK IF YOU LET IT WORK.

134. MINDS ARE LIKE PARACHUTES - THEY WON'T WORK UNLESS THEY'RE OPEN.

135. WHAT YOU SEE AND HEAR HERE, STAYS HERE.

136. ADDICTION IS THE ONLY DISEASE THAT TELLS YOU THAT YOU'RE ALL RIGHT.

137. IF YOU TURN IT OVER AND DON'T LET GO OF IT YOU WILL BE UPSIDE DOWN.

138. A RECOVERY MEETING IS WHERE LOSERS GET TOGETHER TO TALK ABOUT THEIR WINNINGS.

139. THE FELLOWSHIP IS A SCHOOL IN WHICH WE ARE ALL STUDENTS AND ALL TEACHERS.

140. GOD TAUGHT US TO LAUGH AGAIN AND WE ASK GOD TO PLEASE DON'T LET US FORGET THAT WE ONCE CRIED.

141. SERENITY IS NOT FREEDOM FROM THE STORM, BUT PEACE AMID THE STORM.

142. THE "BASIC TEXT" MAY NOT BE ABLE TO SOLVE ALL YOUR PROBLEMS, BUT THE FELLOWSHIP OF RECOVERY IS READY AND WILLING TO HELP YOU FIND A SOLUTION TO THEM.

143. IT ISN'T THE LOAD THAT WEIGHS US DOWN - IT'S THE WAY THAT WE CARRY IT.

144. PRINCIPLES BEFORE PERSONALITIES

145. WHEN YOU DO ALL THE TALKING YOU ONLY LEARN WHAT YOU ALREADY KNOW.

146. THE SEVEN "T'S" OF RECOVERY: TAKE TIME TO THINK THE THING THROUGH.

147. THERE ARE NONE TOO DUMB FOR THE PROGRAM, BUT MANY ARE TOO SMART.

148. WE ALL HAVE ANOTHER RUN IN US, BUT WE DON'T KNOW IF WE HAVE ANOTHER RECOVERY IN US.

149. TO RECEIVE FORGIVENESS, WE MUST LEARN TO FORGIVE.

150. WHEN WE SURRENDER TO OUR HIGHER POWER, THE JOURNEY BEGINS.

151. THE PERSON WITH THE MOST RECOVERY AT A MEETING IS THE ONE WHO GOT UP THE EARLIEST THAT MORNING.

152. KNOWLEDGE OF "THE ANSWERS" NEVER MADE ANYONE GO BACK OUT - IT WAS FAILING TO PRACTICE "THE ANSWERS" THAT WERE KNOWN.

153. H.A.L.T.: DON'T LET YOURSELF GET TOO "HUNGRY," TOO "ANGRY," TOO "LONELY," OR TOO "TIRED," BECAUSE THESE ARE THE BEGINNINGS OF A RELAPSE; BE "HAPPY," "APPRECIATIVE," "LOVABLE," AND "TEACHABLE."

154. RECOVERY WON'T KEEP YOU FROM GOING TO HELL, NOR IS IT A TICKET TO HEAVEN, BUT IT WILL KEEP YOU CLEAN LONG ENOUGH FOR YOU TO MAKE UP YOUR MIND WHICH WAY YOU WANT TO GO.

155. WHEN A PERSON TRIES TO CONTROL THEIR USING, THEY HAVE ALREADY LOST CONTROL.

156. THE TASK AHEAD OF US IS NEVER AS GREAT AS THE POWER BEHIND US.

157. SEVEN DAYS WITHOUT A MEETING MAKES ONE WEAK.

158. YOU ARE NOT REQUIRED TO LIKE IT; YOU ARE ONLY REQUIRED TO DO IT.

159. WHEN WALLOWING IN YOUR SELF-PITY, PLEASE GET OFF THE CROSS BECAUSE WE NEED THE WOOD.

160. WE IN RECOVERY CARRY THE MESSAGE, NOT THE PROBLEM.

161. THE RESULTS OF OUR PRAYERS ARE IN GOD'S HANDS.

162. WE ARE NOT HUMAN BEINGS HAVING SPIRITUAL EXPERIENCES, BUT SPIRITUAL BEINGS HAVING HUMAN EXPERIENCES.

163. REMEMBER THAT NOTHING IS GOING TO HAPPEN TODAY THAT YOU AND YOUR HIGHER POWER CANNOT HANDLE.

164. WHEN MAN LISTENS, GOD SPEAKS AND WHEN MAN OBEYS, GOD WORKS.

165. DO NOT WATCH THE "SLIPPERS," BUT WATCH THOSE WHO DO NOT SLIP CLOSELY AND YOU WILL SEE THEM GO THROUGH DIFFICULTIES AND PULL THROUGH.

166. THE TWO "T'S" IN GRATITUDE ARE WHAT WE GIVE AWAY TO REMAIN CLEAN: OUR TIME AND OUR TREASURE.

167. IT IS A PITY THAT WE CANNOT FORGET OUR TROUBLES THE SAME WAY THAT WE FORGET OUR BLESSINGS.

168. BE CAREFUL WHAT YOU PRAY FOR BECAUSE YOU MAY GET IT.

169. THE TIME TO ATTEND A MEETING IS WHEN YOU LEAST FEEL LIKE GOING TO ONE.

170. WORK THE PROGRAM FROM THE WAIST UP.

171. THE FELLOWSHIP IS THE HIGHEST PRICED CLUB IN THE WORLD, SO, IF YOU HAVE PAID THE DUES, THEN WHY NOT ENJOY THE BENEFITS.

172. THE FIRST STEP IS THE ONLY STEP THAT YOU CAN DO PERFECTLY EACH DAY.

173. THE WILL OF GOD WILL NEVER TAKE YOU WHERE THE GRACE OF GOD WILL NOT PROTECT YOU.

174. YOUR "BASIC TEXT" IS YOUR SPONSOR TOO.

175. THE ROOMS OF THE FELLOWSHIP NEVER OPENED THE GATES OF HEAVEN TO LET YOU IN, BUT THEY DID OPEN THE GATES OF HELL TO LET YOU OUT.

176. THE ONLY THING WE TAKE FROM THIS WORLD WHEN WE LEAVE IT IS WHAT WE GIVE AWAY.

177. TIME WASTED IN GETTING EVEN CAN NEVER BE USED IN GETTING AHEAD.

178. SOME PEOPLE ARE SO SUCCESSFUL IN RECOVERY THAT THEY TURN OUT TO BE ALMOST AS GOOD AS THEY USED TO THINK THEY WERE WHEN THEY WERE USING.

179. RECOVERY DELIVERS EVERYTHING THAT USING PROMISED.

180. POSSIBILITIES AND MIRACLES ARE ONE IN THE SAME.

181. GET OUT OF THE DRIVER'S SEAT - LET GO AND LET GOD.

182. H.O.W.: HONESTY, OPEN-MINDEDNESS, AND WILLINGNESS.

183. A DANGER SIGN: WHEN YOUR EYES HAVE WANDERED FROM THE PERSON WHO STILL SUFFERS AND NEEDS HELP.

184. FIRST WE STAYED CLEAN BECAUSE WE HAD TO, THEN WE STAYED CLEAN BECAUSE WE WERE WILLING TO, AND NOW WE STAY CLEAN BECAUSE WE WANT TO.

185. SLOGANS ARE WISDOM WRITTEN IN SHORTHAND.

186. THOSE IN ACTIVE ADDICTION DO NOT HAVE RELATIONSHIPS – THEY HAVE HOSTAGES.

187. EVERY DAY IS A GIFT AND THAT IS WHY WE CALL IT THE PRESENT.

188. IF YOU FIND A PATH WITH NO OBSTACLES, IT PROBABLY DOESN'T LEAD ANYWHERE.

189. EACH AND EVERY RECOVERY FROM ADDICTION BEGAN WITH A SINGLE CLEAN HOUR.

190. EACH AND EVERY PERSON IN THE ROOMS, CLEAN OR NOT, TEACHES US SOME VALUABLE LESSON ABOUT OURSELVES.

191. WE HAD TO QUIT PLAYING GOD.

192. DON'T COMPARE - IDENTIFY.

193. DON'T INTELLECTUALIZE - UTILIZE.

194. DON'T TAKE YOURSELF SO DAMN SERIOUSLY.

195. RECOVERY IS LIKE AN ADJUSTABLE WRENCH IN THAT IT WILL FIT EACH AND EVERY NUT THAT WALKS THROUGH A MEETING ROOM DOOR.

196. LIVE IN THE HERE AND NOW.

197. DON'T PICK UP + DON'T DIE = ONE "OLD TIMER."

198. THE FELLOWSHIP SPOILS YOUR USING.

199. FAITH IS OUR GREATEST GIFT AND SHARING IS OUR GREATEST RESPONSIBILITY.

200. IF YOU WANT TO GO BACK OUT THAT IS YOUR BUSINESS AND IF YOU WANT TO QUIT THAT IS THE FELLOWSHIP'S BUSINESS.

201. IN A BAR WE GET SYMPATHY AS LONG AS OUR MONEY WILL LAST, BUT IN THE ROOMS WE GET EMPATHY FOR NOTHING.

202. EVEN YOUR WORST DAY IN RECOVERY IS BETTER THAN YOUR BEST DAY USING.

203. THE ELEVATOR IS BROKEN, PLEASE USE THE STEPS.

204. LET IT BEGIN WITH ME.

205. WHEN ALL ELSE FAILS, REMEMBER THE DIRECTIONS ARE IN THE "BASIC TEXT."

206. TRUST GOD + CLEAN HOUSE + HELP OTHERS = LONG-TERM RECOVERY.

207. ANONYMITY IS SO IMPORTANT THAT WE CAN USE IT AS OUR LAST NAME.

208. IF WE DON'T GROW, THEN WE'RE GOING TO GO.

209. ALL YOU NEED TO START ANOTHER MEETING IS A RESENTMENT AND A COFFEE POT.

210. RELIGION IS FOR THOSE WHO FEAR GOD AND SPIRITUALITY IS FOR THOSE WHO HAVE BEEN TO HELL AND BACK.

211. THERE ARE NO ATHEISTS IN FOXHOLES.

212. THREE SUGGESTIONS FOR MAKING A SPEECH: BE INTERESTING, BE BRIEF, AND THEN BE SEATED.

213. WHEN YOU ARE A SPONSOR YOU GET OUT OF YOURSELF: IF I SERVE I WILL BE SERVED.

214. WHY RECOVERY NEVER ENDS: THE DISEASE IS CALLED ALCOHOLISM, NOT ALCOHOLWASM.

215. THE RECOVERY WAY OF LIFE IS MEANT TO BE BREAD FOR OUR DAILY USE AND NOT CAKE FOR SPECIAL OCCASIONS.

216. THE SMARTEST THING A MEMBER OF THE FELLOWSHIP CAN EVER SAY IS, "HELP ME."

217. THE STUPIDEST QUESTION A MEMBER CAN EVER HAVE IS THE ONE NEVER ASKED.

218. YOU ARE EXACTLY WHERE GOD WANTS YOU TO BE.

219. GOD WILL NEVER GIVE YOU MORE THAN YOU CAN HANDLE.

220. SLOW BUT SURE.

221. IN RECOVERY WE SAY THAT A "COINCIDENCE" IS A MIRACLE IN WHICH GOD CHOOSES TO REMAIN ANONYMOUS.

222. IT TAKES THE GOOD AND BAD MEETING AND THE GOOD AND BAD TALK TO MAKE THIS FELLOWSHIP WORK.

223. GIVE T.I.M.E. (THINGS I MUST EARN) TIME.

224. GIVE T.I.M.E. THE TIME THAT IT NEEDS.

225. FAITH IS A LIGHTED DOORWAY, BUT TRUST IS
A DARK HALL.

226. THE MOST IMPORTANT LESSON WE LEARN IN
RECOVERY IS SIMPLY THAT OUR SPIRITUAL
LIFE IS LIMITED TO OUR OWN BEHAVIOR AND
ATTITUDE.

227. THE PARADOXES OF RECOVERY ARE:
FROM WEAKNESS (ADVERSITY) COMES STRENGTH,
FROM DARKNESS COMES LIGHT,
FROM DEPENDENCE COMES INDEPENDENCE,
WE FORGIVE TO BE FORGIVEN,
WE GIVE IT AWAY TO KEEP IT,
WE SUFFER TO GET WELL,
WE SURRENDER TO WIN, AND
WE DIE TO LIVE.

AUTHOR UNKNOWN

228. RECOVERY WORKS FOR PEOPLE WHO BELIEVE IN
A HIGHER POWER AND RECOVERY WORKS FOR
PEOPLE WHO DO NOT BELIEVE IN A HIGHER POWER,
BUT RECOVERY WILL NEVER WORK FOR PEOPLE WHO
BELIEVE THAT THEY ARE A HIGHER POWER.

229. THERE ARE TWO DAYS IN EVERY WEEK IN WHICH
WE CANNOT MAKE ANY CHANGES TO OUR LIVES
AND THAT IS YESTERDAY AND TOMORROW.
THEREFORE, TODAY IS THE ONLY DAY THAT WE
ARE CONCERNED WITH.

230. IT IS THE REMORSE AND BITTERNESS FOR
SOMETHING THAT HAPPENED YESTERDAY AS
WELL AS THE DREAD OF WHAT TOMORROW MAY
BRING THAT DRIVES A PERSON OUT OF THE ROOMS
AND NOT THE EXPERIENCE OF TODAY.

231. SLIPPERS IN THE ROOMS UTILIZE THE REVOLVING
DOOR POLICY.

232. PAIN IS THE TOUCHSTONE OF SPIRITUAL GROWTH.

233. GOD HAS NO GRAND CHILDREN, STEP CHILDREN, NIECES, OR NEPHEWS.

234. THERE IS A GOD AND I AM NOT HIM.

235. THE ROAD TO DISAPPOINTMENT (RESENTMENT) IS PAVED WITH EXPECTATION.

236. BE NICE TO NEWCOMERS FOR ONE DAY ONE OF THEM MAY BE YOUR SPONSOR.

237. DENIAL IS NOT A RIVER IN EGYPT.

238. GUILT IS A GIFT THAT KEEPS ON GIVING.

239. THE FLIP SIDE TO FORGIVENESS IS A RESENTMENT.

240. THERE IS NO MAGIC IN RECOVERY - ONLY MIRACLES.

241. FEAR IS THE ABSENCE OF FAITH.

242. COURAGE IS FAITH THAT HAS SAID ITS PRAYERS.

243. DEPRESSION IS ANGER TURNED INWARD.

244. THOSE IN RECOVERY HEAL FROM THE OUTSIDE IN, BUT FEEL FROM THE INSIDE OUT.

245. THE THREE A'S OF RECOVERY: AFFECTION (THOUGHTFULNESS), ATTENTION (LISTENING), AND APPRECIATION (GRATITUDE).

246. IF IT IS MEANT TO BE THEN I CANNOT STOP IT AND IF IT IS NOT GOD'S WILL THEN I CANNOT MAKE IT HAPPEN.

247. THERE ARE PEOPLE IN RECOVERY WHO MAKE THINGS HAPPEN AND THERE ARE PEOPLE IN RECOVERY WHO WATCH THINGS HAPPEN AND THEN THERE ARE PEOPLE IN THE ROOMS WHO DON'T KNOW IF ANYTHING IS HAPPENING AT ALL.

248. BELIEVE SIMPLY BECAUSE WE BELIEVE.

249. F.E.A.R.: FALSE EVIDENCE APPEARING REAL.

250. H.I.G.H.: HOPE IS GIVEN HERE.

251. DON'T PICK UP TODAY AND TOMARROW WILL TAKE
CARE OF ITSELF.

252. PUT THE PLUG IN THE JUG AND THROW IT AWAY.

253. I DIDN'T QUIT, I SURRENDERED.

254. IT'S SUPER BEING SOBER.

255. IT WORKS IF YOU LET IT.

256. LIVE .... EASY .... BUT .... THINK .... FIRST.
    AND   DOES   FOR   THINK   THINGS
    LET   IT.   THE   THINK.   FIRST.
    LIVE.   GRACE
                           OF
                           GOD.

257. P.T.S.D.: PURGING THOSE STUPID DRUGS.

258. GOD IS NOT LOST SO YOU CAN STOP LOOKING
FOR HIM.

259. IF YOU DON'T GO WITHIN THEN YOU'LL GO WITHOUT.

260. EVERY SUCCESS IS A FAILURE AND EVERY FAILURE
IS A SUCCESS.

261. YOU CAN'T THINK YOUR WAY INTO GOOD LIVING,
BUT YOU CAN LIVE YOUR WAY INTO GOOD THINKING.

262. Y.E.T.: YOU'RE ELIGIBLE TOO.

263. D.R.I.N.K.: DROWNING RESULTS IN NOT KNOWING;
DEATH RESULTS IN NOT KNOWING.

264. S.T.E.P.S.: SOLUTIONS TO EVERY PROBLEM SOBER.

265. T.H.I.N.K.: THE HAPPINESS I NOW KNOW.

266. S.C.U.D.: SICKNESS CONTINUOUSLY USES
DISTRACTIONS.

267. C.O.F.F.E.E.: COMING OVER, FINDING FRIENDS, EXPRESSING EMOTIONS.

268. P.R.O.G.R.A.M.: PEOPLE RELYING ON GOD RELAYING A MESSAGE.

269. S.P.O.N.S.O.R.: SOBER PERSON OFFERING NEWCOMER SOLUTIONS ON RECOVERY.

270. A.I.R.: ACTION IS RECOVERY.

271. H.O.P.E.: HAVING OUR PROBLEMS ERASED; HAPPY OUR PROGRAM EXISTS; HAVING OUR PRAYERS EVOLVE; HELPING OTHER PEOPLE EVERYDAY.

272. G.O.D.: GOOD ORDERLY DIRECTION; GREAT OVERSEER DIRECTING; GRACE OVER DEATH; GATHERING OF DRUNKS.

273. MAKE PLANS FOR THE FUTURE, BUT DON'T PLAN THE OUTCOME.

274. IN RECOVERY "SKID ROW" IS NOT A GEOGRAPHICAL LOCATION - IT LIES BETWEEN OUR EARS.

275. PUT YOUR RECOVERY IN YOUR HEART AND NOT IN YOUR HEAD BECAUSE THAT IS WHERE YOUR DISEASE LIVES.

276. YOUR HIGHER POWER WILL NOT CLOSE THE DOOR BEHIND YOU WITHOUT OPENING A DOOR AHEAD OF YOU, BUT YOU MAY HAVE TO WAIT IN THE HALL BEFORE YOU CAN ENTER.

277. THE PERSON IN THE GLASS KNOWS JUST HOW SICK YOU REALLY ARE.

278. WE WILL LOVE YOU UNCONDITIONALLY BECAUSE YOU ARE IN THE ROOMS, BUT WE DON'T HAVE TO LOVE THE THINGS THAT YOU SAY OR DO.

279. JUST BECAUSE I'M IN RECOVERY DOESN'T MEAN THAT I HAVE TO BE A DOORMAT TO ANYONE!

280. AN HONEST PROGRAM GIVES US SOBRIETY, PEACE OF MIND, AND CONFIDENCE IN THE FUTURE.

281. N.U.T.S.: NOT USING THE STEPS.

282. THE ONLY MEETING THAT YOU ARE EVER LATE FOR IS YOUR FIRST ONE.

283. DON'T LET YOUR PAST BECOME YOUR FUTURE.

284. SECONDS = MINUTES = HOURS = DAYS = WEEKS = MONTHS = YEARS.

285. EVERY TIME WE PICK UP ITS LIKE GETTING ON AN ELEVATOR THAT ONLY HAS A DOWN BUTTON – YOU NEVER KNOW IF OR WHEN YOU WILL BE GETTING OFF.

286. IF YOU FEEL AS IF YOUR ASS IS COMING APART GET IT TO A MEETING AND WE'LL HELP YOU GET IT TOGETHER AGAIN.

287. DON'T GO INTO YOUR HEAD WITHOUT YOUR SPONSOR'S SUPERVISION.

288. RECOVERY IS NOT A RACE - IT'S A JOURNEY.

289. IF YOU HAVE TO LOOK INTO A MIRROR TO SPEAK TO YOUR SPONSOR THEN YOU'RE IN BIG TROUBLE.

290. IN RECOVERY GROWTH IS MAKING NEW MISTAKES AND LEARNING FROM THEM.

291. KEEP DOING WHAT YOU'RE DOING AND YOU'LL KEEP GETTING WHAT YOU'RE GETTING.

292. IN THE FELLOWSHIP WE'LL LOVE YOU UNTIL YOU LEARN TO LOVE YOURSELF.

293. IF YOU CAN TALK THE TALK, THEN YOU SHOULD WALK THE WALK.

294. WE DO IT IN GROUPS.

295. MISERY IS OPTIONAL.

296. THE RECOVERY HONOR SYSTEM: WORKING THE STEPS TO THE BEST OF YOUR ABILITY.

297. ACTIONS SPEAK LOUDER THAN WORDS.

298. GIVE US JUST ONE YEAR OF YOUR TIME AND IF YOU'RE NOT SATISFIED THAT YOU HAVE BEGUN A BETTER WAY OF LIFE THEN WE'LL GLADLY REFUND YOUR MISERY…IN FULL.

299. GOD DON'T MAKE NO JUNK.

300. THE CORE OF THE DISEASE OF ALCOHOLISM IS THE "I," "SELF," AND "ME."

301. IF YOUR "I'S" ARE TOO CLOSE TOGETHER THEN YOU HAVE PASSED THE SELF-CENTEREDNESS TEST.

302. THERE'S A SLIP UNDER EVERY SKIRT.

303. G.U.T.S.: GUIDANCE USING THE STEPS.

304. YOU CAN'T BLAME ANY ONE BUT YOURSELF IF YOU STUMBLE TWICE OVER THE SAME STONE.

305. ACQUIRE THE HABIT OF BEING FAITHFUL TO FRIENDSHIPS AND RESPONSIBILITIES.

306. THE GREATEST PLEASURE IN LIFE IS TO DO A GOOD TURN IN SECRET AND HAVE IT DISCOVERED BY ACCIDENT.

307. IF YOUR REALITY CHECK BOUNCES YOU'RE LIVING IN A FANTASY WORLD.

308. WOULD YOU LIKE SOME CHEESE WITH THAT WHINE?

309. YOU CAN'T GET RECOVERY THROUGH OSMOSIS.

310. THERE ARE NO BIG "I'S" OR LITTLE "YOU'S" IN RECOVERY.

311. FIRST IT GETS GOOD, THEN IT GETS REAL, AND
THEN IT GETS REAL GOOD.

312. GOD GAVE US FREEWILL, SO IT'S UP TO US TO STAY
CLEAN ONE DAY AT A TIME.

313. ALL IS RIGHT NO MATTER HOW WRONG IT IS.

314. KEEP YOUR EYES ON THE PRIZE.

315. MORE WILL BE REVEALED.

316. THE AGE AT WHICH YOU FIRST PICKED UP + THE
AMOUNT OF RECOVERY TIME THAT YOU HAVE =
YOUR SPIRITUAL AGE.

317. WHEN THE BLAMING STOPS THE HEALING BEGINS.

318. DO THE 180 BECAUSE RESISTANCE TO CHANGE
CAUSES PAIN.

319. WALK SELF AND FLY TO THE MOON.

320. ONCE YOU PICKLE A CUCUMBER IT WILL ALWAYS
BE A PICKLE.

321. IF YOU TAKE THE RUM OUT OF A FRUIT CAKE YOU'LL
STILL HAVE A FRUITCAKE.

322. THE FELLOWSHIP IS FOR QUITTERS.

323. PLAN THE FISHING TRIP, BUT DON'T PLAN
THE CATCH.

324. WHEN THE STUDENT IS READY, THEN THE TEACHER
WILL APPEAR.

325. IF YOU KEEP GOING TO THE "BARBER SHOP"...
SOONER OR LATER YOU'LL GET YOUR HAIR CUT.

326. EMBARRASSMENT IS THE RESPONSE FROM A
PERSON WHO STILL HAS AN EGO INVESTMENT
IN WHAT OTHERS THINK OF THEM.

327. TO TRULY KNOW GOD YOU HAVE TO BE OUT OF YOUR MIND.

328. IF YOU DON'T GO WITHIN, THEN YOU'LL GO WITHOUT.

329. YOU DON'T THROW A WHOLE LIFE AWAY JUST BECAUSE IT'S BANGED UP A LITTLE.

330. GOD'S WILL: TREAT YOURSELF WITH RESPECT, TREAT OTHERS WITH RESPECT, AND LIVE THE MESSAGE OF RECOVERY.

331. JUST ACCEPT, DON'T EXPECT.

332. ACCEPTANCE IS KNOWING THE PAST WILL NEVER GET BETTER.

333. EXPERIENCE IS WHAT YOU GET WHEN YOU DON'T GET WHAT YOU WANT.

334. LIFE IS 10% OF WHAT YOU MAKE IT AND 90% OF HOW YOU TAKE IT.

335. STOP BARKING AND START BITING.

336. THEY'RE NOT DOING IT TO YOU, THEY'RE JUST DOING IT.

337. YOU CAN'T CHANGE THE WIND, BUT YOU CAN ADJUST YOUR SAILS.

338. ACTION ALLEVIATES ANXIETY.

339. LAZY WORKS TWICE.

340. YOU HAVE TO ACT RIGHT IN ORDER TO FEEL RIGHT.

341. AN ALCOHOLIC WILL STEAL YOUR WALLET, BUT AN ADDICT WILL STEAL YOUR WALLET AND THEN HELP YOU LOOK FOR IT.

342. THE QUICKER, THE SICKER, THE SOONER, THE BETTER.

343. OUR DISEASE MAKES US SOMEONE WHO WANTS TO BE HELD WHILE ISOLATING.

344. AN ALCOHOLIC ONLY LIKES TO DRINK ON DAYS THAT BEGIN WITH A "T": TUESDAY, THURSDAY, TODAY, AND TOMORROW.

345. STINKING THINKING: "I MAY NOT BE MUCH, BUT I'M ALL THAT I LIKE TO THINK ABOUT."

346. IF IT LOOKS LIKE A "DUCK," SOUNDS LIKE A "DUCK," AND WALKS LIKE A "DUCK," THEN IT MUST BE A . . . "DUCK."

347. IF YOU DRANK ENOUGH TO GET INTO RECOVERY, THEN YOU DRANK ENOUGH.

348. ALCOHOL PROVOKES THE DESIRE, AND THEN TAKES AWAY THE PERFORMANCE.

349. IT'S NOT WHAT BRAND OF ALCOHOL YOU DRANK OR HOW MUCH YOU DRANK, IT'S WHAT IT DID TO YOU THAT COUNTS.

350. ALCOHOLIC: A PERSON SUFFERING FROM TERMINAL UNIQUENESS.

351. THEY DIDN'T MAKE A GLASS BIG ENOUGH FOR ME TO HAVE JUST ONE DRINK.

352. AN ALCOHOLIC ALONE IS SLUMMING.

353. AN ALCOHOLIC ISN'T A GUY WHO THINKS HE'S HAD ONE TOO MANY, HE'S THE GUY WHO THINKS HE'S HAD ONE TOO FEW.

354. BEING "A LITTLE BIT ALCOHOLIC" IS LIKE BEING "A LITTLE BIT PREGNANT."

355. AN ALCOHOLICS FAVORITE BRAND IS "MORE."

356. IF YOU THINK THAT YOU'RE SICK, THE CHANCES ARE THAT YOU ARE.

357. P.U.S.H.: PRAY UNTIL SOMETHING HAPPENS.

358. B.A.R.: BEWARE, ALCOHOL, RUN.

359. IT TAKES WHAT IT TAKES TO GET INTO THE ROOMS AND IT TAKES WHAT IT TAKES TO STAY IN THE ROOMS.

360. THE DESTINY OF EVERY ALCOHOLIC IS TO BE LOCKED UP, COVERED UP, OR SOBERED UP.

361. YOU CAN CARRY THE MESSAGE, BUT NOT THE PERSON WHO NEEDS TO HEAR IT.

362. DREAMS THAT WE GAVE UP ON CAN BECOME REALITIES.

363. DEFECTS GROW IN THE DARK AND DIE IN THE LIGHT.

364. COMPLETELY CHANGE YOUR OLD WAYS OR GO BACK TO WHAT YOU WERE DOING.

365. BY SURRENDERING CONTROL WE GAIN A FAR GREATER POWER.

366. PRO-CRAS-TIN-A-TION IS A FIVE SYLLABLE WORD FOR SLOTH.

367. IF YOU THINK THAT SPILLING BEER IS ALCOHOL ABUSE, THEN YOU'RE PROBABLY AN ALCOHOLIC.

368. ALCOHOLICS ARE IN A CLASS ALL BY THEMSELVES BECAUSE EVERYONE ELSE HAS GRADUATED.

369. HIGH BOTTOMS CAN HAVE TRAP DOORS.

370. IF THE TREATMENT WORKS, THEN CHANCES ARE THAT YOU HAVE THE DISEASE.

371. WE ARE NOT REFORMED DRUNKS – BUT INFORMED ALCOHOLICS.

372. WE ARE HERE FOR A REASON, NOT FOR A SEASON.

373. EVERY GROUP WILL BE JUDGED BY THE ACTIONS OF THE WORST OF ITS MEMBERS.

374. WHEN YOU CLEAN UP YOUR MEETING ROOM BEFORE YOU LEAVE, YOU LEAVE THE SIGNATURE OF RECOVERY BEHIND YOU.

375. THE ROOMS ARE NOT A SENTENCE, THEY ARE A REPRIEVE.

376. A.A.: ATTITUDE ADJUSTMENT; ALTERED ATTITUDES; ACKNOWLEDGE ACCEPTANCE; AVOID ANGER.

377. SERVICE WORK BEGINS AT YOUR HOME GROUP AND YOUR HOME.

378. "DARE AND MEDICATION" OR "PRAYER AND MEDITATION."

379. IF THE CURE WORKS, CHANCES ARE, THAT YOU HAVE THE DISEASE.

380. IN LOVING YOU, UNCONDITIONALLY, I AM LOSING THE OLD ME.

381. THE THREE MOST DANGEROUS WORDS FOR A NEWCOMER ARE: "I'VE BEEN THINKING."

382. WE ARE NOT BAD PEOPLE BECOMING GOOD, BUT SICK PEOPLE BECOMING WELL.

383. YOUR NEXT BOTTOM MAY BE SIX FEET UNDER.

384. ALCOHOLISM DOES NOT COME IN BOTTLES, IT COMES IN PEOPLE.

385. ALCOHOLISM IS A SELF-DIAGNOSED DISEASE.

386. SOME PEOPLE THINK ALCOHOLISM IS A TWO-FOLD DISEASE: MORE AND RIGHT NOW.

387. A.L.E.: ALIBIS, LIES, AND EXCUSES.

388. THE SPIRITUAL PART OF MY DISEASE TELLS ME THAT I CAN GO FROM GRATEFUL TO HATEFUL IN A SECOND.

389. PAUSE WHEN AGITATED OR PAWS WHEN AGITATED.

390. WE ARE ONLY AS BIG AS THE SMALLEST THING THAT CAN MAKE US ANGRY.

391. ANGER IS BUT A MASK FOR FEAR.

392. THOSE WHO ANGER YOU CAN CONQUER YOU.

393. THE NEWCOMER DOES NOT SAY THINGS JUST TO MAKE YOU ANGRY, THEY SAY THINGS THAT MAKE YOU ANGRY.

394. A+T+T+I+T+U+D+E (1 THRU 26 LETTERS IN THE ALPHABET) = 1+20+20+9+20+21+4+5 = 100% SICK.

395. YOU CAN WAKE UP AND SAY, "GOOD GOD, IT'S MORNING," OR "GOOD MORNING, GOD."

396. YOU GET WHAT "YOU" EXPECT IN LIFE.

397. DON'T COUNT THE DAYS, MAKE THE DAYS COUNT.

398. SOMETIMES OUR PAST IS LIKE A TRACTOR PULLING A TRAILER IN THAT IT WILL ALWAYS BE WITH US UNTIL WE LET IT GO.

399. RECOVERY IS NOT MY WHOLE LIFE, BUT IT MADE MY LIFE WHOLE.

400. THOSE THAT JUDGE DON'T MATTER, AND THOSE THAT MATTER DON'T JUDGE.

401. A HUMAN BEING IS NOT A HUMAN DOING.

402. IF IT'S TO BE, THEN IT'S UP TO ME.

403. WHAT WILL BE . . . WILL APPEAR.

404. BEING HUMBLE MEANS BEING TEACHABLE.

405. IF YOU WANT TO HIDE SOMETHING FROM A NEWCOMER, PUT IT IN THE "BASIC TEXT."

406. THE "BASIC TEXT" IS ONE OF THOSE RARE BOOKS THAT GETS SMARTER EVERY TIME THAT YOU READ IT.

407. YOU MAY BE THE ONLY COPY OF THE "BASIC TEXT" THAT SOME PEOPLE WILL EVER SEE.

408. DON'T POINT THE FINGER WHEN YOU CAN POINT THE WHOLE HAND BY REACHING OUT.

409. WHEN YOU POINT A FINGER AT SOMEONE YOU HAVE THREE TIMES THAT MANY POINTING BACK AT YOU.

410. MAY YOU BE BLESSED WITH A SLOW RECOVERY.

411. NO ONE COMES INTO THE ROOMS OF RECOVERY FOR THE FIRST TIME ON A GOOD DAY.

412. WHEN THINGS GET WORSE FASTER THAN YOU CAN LOWER YOUR STANDARDS YOU HAVE PROBABLY FOUND YOUR BOTTOM.

413. IF SOMEONE STARTS TO TRY TO PRESS YOUR BUTTONS, PRESS THE "MUTE" ON YOUR REMOTE.

414. PEOPLE IN RECOVERY DON'T CARE HOW MUCH YOU KNOW, UNTIL THEY KNOW HOW MUCH YOU CARE.

415. TAKE CARE OF YOUR RECOVERING MIND AND BODY AND SPIRIT OR BE EVICTED.

416. IF YOU DON'T CHANGE, THEN YOU MAY BE BEGGING FOR LOOSE CHANGE.

417. IF YOU HAVE GOD IN ONE HAND AND THE FELLOWSHIP OF RECOVERY IN THE OTHER HAND, THERE'S A GOOD PROBABILITY THAT YOU WON'T BE ABLE TO PICK UP TODAY.

418. IF YOU KEEP DOING THE SAME THING OVER AND OVER EACH DAY, YOU'LL KEEP GETTING THE SAME THING OVER AND OVER DAILY.

419. IF YOU WANT TO KEEP FEELING HOW YOU'RE FEELING, THEN KEEP DOING WHAT YOU'RE DOING.

420. SUCCESS DOESN'T COME FROM WHAT GOD HAS GIVEN YOU, BUT FROM WHAT YOU DO WITH IT.

421. IF YOU WANT WHAT YOU'VE NEVER HAD, YOU HAVE TO DO WHAT YOU'VE NEVER DONE.

422. RECOVERY BEGINS RIGHT OUTSIDE OF YOUR COMFORT ZONE.

423. PUT DOWN THE SURVIVOR WEAPONS AND PICK UP THE RECOVERY TOOLS.

424. IF YOU FAIL TO CHANGE THE PERSON YOU ARE WHEN YOU COME INTO RECOVERY, THEN THAT PERSON MAY JUST TAKE YOU BACK TO WHERE YOU WERE.

425. LEARN TO CHANGE AND CHANGE TO LEARN.

426. THERE ARE TWO THINGS THAT A NEWCOMER DOESN'T LIKE: THE WAY THAT THINGS ARE AND CHANGE.

427. THE TOPIC IS CALLED "HOW IT WORKS," NOT "WHY ME."

428. IT'S THE THINGS THAT YOU LEARN AFTER YOU KNOW EVERYTHING THAT COUNT.

429. RECOVERY IS GAINED OVER TIME, NOT OVER NIGHT.

430. THERE'S A LOT OF DIS-EASE BETWEEN THE ACCEPTANCE OF WHAT WE HAVE BECOME AND HONESTY, OPEN-MINDEDNESS, AND WILLINGNESS.

431. YOU CAN'T LIVE IN TODAY IF YOUR MIND IS IN YESTERDAY.

432. IF YOU FEEL LIKE YOU'RE GOING THROUGH HELL, PLEASE DON'T STOP WALKING.

433. F.E.A.R.: FRUSTRATION, EGO, ANXIETY, AND RESENTMENT.

434. IF YOU CARRIED A STONE FOR EVERY RESENTMENT THAT YOU HAVE, YOU WOULD SOON LEARN TO LET THEM GO (THE BIGGER THE RESENTMENT, THE BIGGER THE STONE).

435. IF YOU'RE TOO SMART FOR YOUR OWN GOOD YOU MAY BE INTERFERING IN YOUR OWN RECOVERY.

436. IF IT'S TO BE, THEN IT'S UP TO ME.

437. F.A.I.T.H.: FANTASTIC ADVENTURES IN TRUSTING HIM.

438. OUR TRADITIONS ARE LIKE A SILVER PLATTER THAT BRINGS THE STEPS TO US AND IT'S OUR RESPONSIBILITY TO KEEP THE PLATTER POLISHED.

439. STAY A LITTLE GREEN DURING YOUR RECOVERY AND YOU'LL NEVER HAVE TO WORRY ABOUT FALLING FROM THE TREE.

440. LIFE IN RECOVERY IS LIKE A HEART MONITOR WITH ITS UPS AND DOWNS AND IF YOUR LIFE IS A FLAT LINE THEN YOU ARE NOT LIVING - YOU'RE DEAD!

441. HURTING PEOPLE HURT PEOPLE.

442. "JANE HOPS" AND HER FRIEND "JOHN BARLEYCORN" PROMISED ME A LIFE BEYOND MY WILDEST DREAMS AND THEN TOOK AWAY MY REASON FOR LIVING.

443. SURRENDER THE ME FOR THE WE.

444. RECOVERY IS THE PROCESS OF DISCOVERY.

445. "I'M F.I.N.E." (FRUSTRATED, INSECURE, NEUROTIC, AND EMOTIONAL).

446. WHEN A NEWCOMER ASKS, "HOW LONG DO I HAVE TO GO TO THESE DAMN MEETINGS?," THE REPLY WILL PROBABLY BE "WHEN YOU CAN WALK ON WATER."

447. WHEN WE CAME INTO RECOVERY OUR BRAINS NEEDED A WASHING, NOW THEY ONLY NEED A RINSING ONCE IN A WHILE.

448. DON'T LET THE THINGS THAT YOU GAIN DURING YOUR RECOVERY TAKE YOUR RECOVERY AWAY FROM YOU.

449. BEFORE I CAME INTO RECOVERY, I HAD ABOUT 22,000 THOUGHTS A DAY - 21,000 OF WHICH WERE ABOUT PICKING UP AGAIN.

450. FEELINGS ARE THE MOST THAT WE HAVE AND THE LEAST UNDERSTOOD.

451. FEEL IT NOW, FEEL IT LATER, OR DIE FEELING IT.

452. ALCOHOLICS AND ADDICTS ARE OUTCASTS FROM THE MENTAL INSTITUTIONS.

453. H. & I.: HARMONY & INTIMACY.

454. THE FURTHER THAT I GET AWAY FROM MY HIGHER POWER, THE CLOSER I GET TO ANOTHER RUN.

455. ENTERING RECOVERY IS LIKE ENTERING A FOREIGN COUNTRY FOR THE FIRST TIME AND THAT IS WHY WE NEED A HOME GROUP TO "WORK" OUT OF AND A SPONSOR TO "GUIDE" US IN THE RIGHT DIRECTION.

456. "YOU HAVE POTENTIAL" DEFINED: "YOU AIN'T DONE SHIT YET."

457. THE FOURTH STEP IS LIKE PEELING AN ONION LAYER BY LAYER.

458. IF YOU CAN'T TAKE CARE OF YOURSELF, WHY SHOULD ANYONE ELSE?

459. WINNERS DO WHAT THEY HAVE TO DO AND LOSERS DO WHAT THEY WANT TO DO.

460. HOW I FEEL IS RARELY AN INDICATION OF HOW I'M DOING.

461. MOST GOOD IDEAS ARE SIMPLE.

462. DON'T BELIEVE EVERYTHING THAT YOU THINK.

463. DON'T PUSH A NEWCOMER TOO FAST BECAUSE A HEAVY DOWNPOUR RUNS OFF AND A GENTLE RAIN SOAKS IN.

464. CONQUER YOURSELF RATHER THAN THE WORLD.

465. THE MORE THAT YOU HAVE ON THE INSIDE, THE LESS YOU NEED ON THE OUTSIDE.

466. THE FIRST THING THAT YOU PUT BEFORE YOUR RECOVERY IS THE FIRST THING THAT YOU'LL LOOSE.

467. SHARING: IF YOU PASS, IT'S YOUR ASS.

468. IN RELATIONSHIPS IT'S NOT A QUESTION OF FINDING THE RIGHT PERSON, BUT BECOMING THE RIGHT PERSON.

469. DON'T WRITE "SCRIPTS" (PRESCRIPTIONS OR PLAYS) UNLESS YOU'RE GOING TO PUBLISH THEM.

470. PRIOR PLANNING PREVENTS PROBLEMS.

471. "NONALCOHOLIC" BEER IS FOR NONALCOHOLICS.

472. A MEETING LASTS FROM PREAMBLE TO PRAYER.

473. IT ISN'T WHAT I DON'T KNOW THAT GETS ME INTO TROUBLE; IT'S WHAT I ABSOLUTELY DO KNOW – AND JUST ISN'T SO.

474. IT DOESN'T MATTER SO MUCH WHO IS RIGHT, BUT WHAT IS RIGHT.

475. THIS ISN'T HAPPENING "TO" YOU, IT'S HAPPENING "FOR" YOU.

476. IS IT ODD OR IS IT GOD.

477. SWITCHING FROM ALCOHOL TO ANOTHER DRUG, OR VISA VERSA, IS LIKE CHANGING ROOMS ON THE TITANIC.

478. THE FIRST DRINK IS THE ONE THAT WILL KILL YOU. IT IS LIKE A TRAIN IN THAT THE LOCOMOTIVE KILLS YOU AND THE CARS THAT FOLLOW JUST HELP CARRY YOUR BODY DOWN THE TRACK.

479. ESTEEM: MY NET WORTH IS NOT MY SELF WORTH.

480. I CAME FOR MY DRINKING AND STAYED FOR MY THINKING.

481. IT'S A CINCH BY THE INCH AND HARD BY THE YARD.

482. IF WE DON'T STAY FOCUSED ON OUR SPIRITUAL GROWTH, THE FURTHER WE'LL GET AWAY FROM OUR LAST RUN AND THE CLOSER WE GET TO OUR NEXT RUN.

483. COMPLACENCY KILLS.

484. OFFER SUGGESTIONS, BUT DON'T TRY TO CHANGE THE OTHER PERSON.

485. WE CAN DISAGREE WITHOUT BEING DISAGREEABLE AND WE CAN ARGUE WITHOUT BEING DIFFICULT.

486. IF YOU HAVE TO CONTROL YOUR DRINKING OR DRUGGING, IT MUST BE OUT OF CONTROL.

487. IF YOU HAVE TO CONTROL YOUR USING, WHAT'S THE POINT OF USING?

488. EXPECTATIONS ARE PREMEDITATED RESENTMENTS.

489. THE FIRST TIME SOBER IS A GIFT; WHY WASTE IT?

490. LISTEN TO YOUR HEART OFTEN BECAUSE GOD LIVES THERE.

491. IF OUR HIGHER POWER IS FOR US, WHO CAN BE AGAINST US?

492. THE BIGGER MY HEAD, THE EASIER THE TARGET.

493. LEARN TO LISTEN AND LISTEN TO LEARN.

494. AFTER EACH MEETING, CLEAN UP THE WRECKAGE OF THE PRESENT.

495. LIVE IN THE MOMENT.

496. EVERYTHING THAT WE HAVE IS ON LOAN FROM GOD.

497. QUITTING IS EASY; IT'S STAYING STOPPED THAT'S HARD.

498. REMEMBER THE THREE "P'S": "PERFECTIONISM" LEADS TO "PROCRASTINATION" WHICH LEADS TO "PARALYSIS."

499. BEEN THERE, DONE THAT, GOT THE T-SHIRT FOR IT.

500. MY DRUG OF CHOICE WAS "MORE."

501. WE CARE.

502. LIFE'S A BEACH AND NOT A BITCH.

503. SOCIAL ACCEPTABILITY DOES NOT EQUAL RECOVERY.

504. MEETING MAKERS MAKE MEETINGS, COFFEE MAKERS MAKE COFFEE, AND STEP TAKERS TAKE STEPS.

505. IN ORDER TO KEEP IT, YOU HAVE TO GIVE IT AWAY.

506. WHEN YOU START TO SKIP, YOU START TO SLIP.

507. HOW WE TREAT OTHERS IS A CONSEQUENCE OF THE DEPTH OF OUR OWN SPIRITUALITY.

508. A "SHORTCOMING" IS LIKE A FLAT TIRE AND A "CHARACTER DEFECT" IS LIKE DRIVING ON IT.

509. YOU CAN BE A HUMAN BEING BUT YOU DON'T HAVE TO BE A HUMAN DOING.

510. THINK IT THROUGH.

511. IF YOU DRINK AT THE BAD NEWS THAT YOU GOT TODAY, YOU'LL NEVER KNOW YOU COULD GET THROUGH IT WITHOUT DRINKING.

512. WINNERS DON'T WHINE AND WHINERS DON'T WIN.

513. IF THERE'S NOTHING WE CAN DO TO PREVENT SOMETHING THEN WE MIGHT AS WELL NOT WORRY ABOUT IT.

514. KEEP COMING BACK NO MATTER WHAT.

515. MY BEST THINKING GOT ME DRUNK.

516. THE BEST WAY FOR ME TO SUCCEED AND GROW IN MY RECOVERY IS TO FOLLOW THE ADVICE I HERE MYSELF GIVING OTHERS.

517. IF YOU ONLY PRAY WHEN YOU NEED SOMETHING FIXED, YOU'RE TURNING GOD INTO A REPAIRMAN.

518. MOST PEOPLE SPEND MORE TIME DECIDING WHERE TO HAVE LUNCH THAN IN CHOOSING A SPONSOR.

519. THE SLIP OCCURS BEFORE YOU PICK UP.

520. SAY WHAT YOU MEAN, BUT DON'T SAY IT MEAN.

521. SOME SAY THAT IF YOU CAN'T REMEMBER YOUR LAST RUN, YOU MAY NOT HAVE HAD IT YET.

522. SURRENDER, DON'T QUIT.

523. STRENGTH IS IN POWERLESSNESS.

524. DO NOT REGRET GROWING OLD BECAUSE IT IS A PRIVILEGE DENIED MANY.

525. IF YOU ONLY NEED ONE MEETING A WEEK YOU MAY HAVE TO GO TO FIVE OF THEM IN THAT TIME TO FIND OUT WHICH ONE IT REALLY IS.

526. LIFE IS FRAGILE: HANDLE WITH CARE.

527. YOU CAN'T SAVE YOUR FACE AND YOUR ASS AT THE SAME TIME.

528. HAPPINESS ISN'T GETTING EVERYTHING YOU WANT BECAUSE IT'S WANTING WHAT YOU'VE ALREADY GOT.

529. THERE IS ONLY ONE THING THAT YOU REALLY NEED TO KNOW ABOUT GOD AND THAT IS THAT YOU ARE NOT HE, SHE, OR IT.

530. KEEP THE FOCUS ON YOURSELF.

531. F.E.A.R.: FORGET EVERYTHING AND RUN; FORGETTING EVERYTHING IS ALL RIGHT; FALSE EVIDENCE APPEARING REAL; FORNICATE EVERYTHING AND RUN; FACE EVERYTHING AND RECOVER.

532. WAKING UP IN STRANGE PLACES WITH STRANGE FACES.

533. NEGATIVITY IS MY DISEASE ASKING ME TO COME OUT AND PLAY.

534. IF WE PUSH DENIAL OUT THE DOOR CHANCES ARE THAT IT WILL TRY TO SNEAK BACK IN THROUGH THE WINDOW: DEAL WITH IT.

535. WHEN YOU DO GOOD, YOU NEVER KNOW HOW MUCH GOOD YOU DO.

536. P.H.D.: POOR HOPELESS DRUNK.

537. FAILURE ISN'T FATAL AND SUCCESS ISN'T PERMANENT.

538. THE PERSON WHO FORGETS IS DOOMED TO REPEAT.

539. TRUST IN GOD TO HELP YOU TRUST IN YOURSELF.

540. HAPPINESS IS AN INSIDE JOB.

541. HUMILITY IS NOT HUMILIATION.

542. LIFE IS ONLY TEMPORARY, SO RELAX AND ENJOY IT.

543. IF YOU THINK THAT YOU DON'T NEED A MEETING, THEN CHANCES ARE THAT YOU DO.

544. DO IT ONE DAY AT A TIME AND REMEMBER THAT THE MIGHTY OAK WAS ONCE A LITTLE NUT THAT HELD IT'S GROUND.

545. GOD HAS A SENSE OF HUMOR SO BE CAREFUL WHAT YOU PRAY FOR - YOU JUST MAY GET IT.

546. ANOTHER DAY, ANOTHER RECOVERY!

547. A RESENTMENT IS LIKE BURNING DOWN YOUR HOUSE TO GET RID OF A RAT.

548. TALK OR DIE.

549. IF YOU WOULD NOT POUR ALCOHOL DOWN THE THROAT OF ANOTHER ALCOHOLIC, WHY WOULD YOU DO IT TO YOURSELF?

550. SLIPS IN LONG-TERM RECOVERY DEFINED: TOO MANY YEARS AND NOT ENOUGH DAYS.

551. PEOPLE WHO SPONSOR THEMSELVES HAVE A SICK PERSON FOR A SPONSOR.

552. I CAN ONLY HELP ANOTHER TO THE DEGREE THAT I'VE BEEN ABLE TO HELP MYSELF.

553. A RICH PERSON IN RECOVERY IS ONE WHO FOLLOWS A SPIRITUAL PATH.

554. THERE WILL COME A TIME, DURING YOUR RECOVERY, WHEN THE ONLY THING BETWEEN YOU AND ANOTHER RUN IS YOUR HIGHER POWER.

555. NOTHING IS SO BAD THAT A DRUG WILL MAKE IT BETTER.

556. IF YOU'RE GOING TO WORRY, WHY PRAY?

557. HERE'S A PERSONAL NOTE FROM GOD: I WILL BE HANDLING ALL OF YOUR PROBLEMS TODAY, SO YOU DON'T HAVE TO WORRY AND I DON'T NEED ANY HELP.

558. THAT WHICH DOESN'T KILL YOU SERVES TO MAKE YOU STRONGER.

559. TODAY IS A VERY IMPORTANT DAY BECAUSE IT'S THE ONLY ONE THAT YOU HAVE.

560. NO PERSON IS A FAILURE WHO HAS FRIENDS IN THE FELLOWSHIP.

561. ONLY IN GIVING DO WE RECEIVE IN FULL MEASURE.

562. TAKE ONE DAY AND ONE STEP AT A TIME AND DON'T EVER LOOK TOO FAR AHEAD.

563. A PERSON IN RECOVERY IS LIKE A TURTLE ON A FENCE POST: YOU KNOW THAT IT HAD HELP.

564. THE OPPOSITE OF LISTENING IS WAITING TO TALK.

565. WHEN YOU ARE LIVING IN SOMEONE'S HEAD THEN YOU ARE OUT OF YOUR MIND.

566. NEVER LOOK BACK TOO LONG UNLESS YOU INTEND TO GO THAT WAY.

567. IF YOU PRAY DON'T WORRY AND IF YOU WORRY DON'T PRAY.

568. THOSE OF THE OPPOSITE SEX MAY PAT YOUR REAR END, BUT OFTEN THOSE OF THE SAME SEX WILL SAVE IT.

569. IF YOU'RE LOOKING FOR GOD, YOU'LL NEVER SEE GOD MORE AT WORK THEN AT A MEETING.

570. LIFE ON LIFE'S TERMS.

571. THE TWELVE STEPS TELL US HOW IT WORKS AND THE TWELVE TRADITIONS TELL US WHY IT WORKS.

572. IF THE DRUGS DON'T KILL YOU, THE LIFESTYLE WILL.

573. HUMILITY IS THAT VIRTUE WHICH REDUCES A MAN TO PROPER SIZE WITHOUT DEGRADING HIM; THEREBY INCREASING HIM IS STATUE WITHOUT INFLATING HIM. UNLESS ONE ATTAINS SOME DEGREE OF HUMILITY, ONE IS CONDEMNED TO MAKE ANOTHER RUN OF IT.

574. HAPPINESS IS APPRECIATING WHAT YOU HAVE AND NOT GETTING WHAT YOU WANT.

575. WE ARE NOT DIFFERENT FROM OTHERS, GOD JUST MADE US SPECIAL.

576. FORGIVENESS OF OTHERS IS A GIFT TO YOURSELF.

577. OUR NUMBER ONE PAIN RELIEVER IS SPELLED F-O-R-G-I-V-E-N-E-S-S.

578. FAITH CAN'T BE TAUGHT BUT IT CAN BE CAUGHT.

579. EGOISM ISN'T NECESSARILY THINKING A LOT OF YOURSELF; IT'S MORE LIKE THINKING OF YOURSELF A LOT.

580. WHEN YOU DON'T KNOW WHAT TO DO, THEN DO NOTHING.

581. THERE ARE TWO KINDS OF PEOPLE IN THIS WORLD – THE DOERS AND THE DONE TOS.

582. ILLEGAL DRUGS VS LEGAL DRUGS: THE ONLY DIFFERENCE IS THE KIND OF BULLET THAT GETS YOU.

583. TRYING IS WHAT KEPT ME OUT THERE AND DOING IS WHAT KEEPS ME IN THE ROOMS.

584. NOBODY GIVES ME A BAD DAY WITHOUT MY PERMISSION.

585. IF YOU STOP TREATING YOURSELF POORLY, IT WILL BECOME UNACCEPTABLE FOR OTHERS TO DO SO.

586. THE HIGHEST SERVICE POSITION I CAN OBTAIN IN THE FELLOWSHIP IS DOOR GREETER.

587. FAITH CONQUERS FEAR.

588. IF YOU DON'T BELIEVE, THEN MAKE BELIEVE.

589. IF I HAVE FAITH IN A HIGHER POWER, IT DOESN'T MAKE MUCH DIFFERENCE IF I HAVE FAITH IN MYSELF.

590. GOD HAS FOUR ANSWERS TO CHOOSE FROM FOR EACH PRAYER: "YES;" "NO;" "LET ME THINK ABOUT IT;" AND "WAIT IN THE HALL."

591. THE JACKPOT PRAYER THAT WE ALL KNOW AND LOVE IS "GOD HELP ME."

592. WHEN GOD MADE TIME, HE MADE PLENTY OF IT.

593. IF YOU ARE NOT HAPPY WITH WHAT YOU HAVE, WHAT MAKES YOU THINK THAT YOU WILL BE HAPPY WITH MORE.

594. IF IT WASN'T FOR A SMALL DEFICIT IN MY HUMILITY, I'D BE PERFECT.

595. GOD GAVE YOU TWO EARS AND ONE MOUTH FOR A VERY SPECIAL REASON.

596. GET SMART FEET AND GO TO MEETINGS OFTEN.

597. IN RECOVERY, YOU ARE GIVEN PERMISSION TO BE ORDINARY.

598. TEARS ARE LIQUID PRAYERS.

599. A DAY WITHOUT PRAYER IS A DAY UNFULFILLED.

600. HIT HIM, HER, OR IT WITH A PRAYER, NOT A CHAIR.

601. I MAY NOT BE WHAT I WANT TO BE, BUT I CERTAINLY AM NOT WHAT I WAS.

602. "RESENTMENT" IS FROM THE LATIN, MEANING TO "FEEL AGAIN."

603. THERE IS PLENTY TO GO AROUND OF WHAT YOU GIVE AWAY.

604. GOD DIDN'T SAVE YOU FROM DROWNING TO BEAT YOU UP ON THE BEACH.

605. GIVE UP (STEPS 1, 2, 3), CLEAN UP (STEPS 4, 5, 6), MAKE UP (STEPS 7, 8, 9), AND KEEP UP (STEPS 10, 11, 12).

606. PRACTICE THESE PRINCIPLES IN ALL YOUR AFFAIRS OR CHANGE YOUR AFFAIRS.

607. WE ARE HARDEST TO LOVE WHEN WE NEED LOVE THE MOST.

608. STEP ONE PLUS STEP TWELVE EQUALS STEP THIRTEEN.

609. SOMETIMES THE WORST THINGS IN LIFE HAPPEN AFTER WE GET WHAT WE THINK THAT WE WANT.

610. THERE ARE NO LOSERS IN RECOVERY.

611. IF YOU KEEP ONE FOOT IN YESTERDAY AND THE OTHER FOOT IN TOMORROW YOU'RE PISSING ALL OVER TODAY.

612. LIVE FOR TODAY BECAUSE TOMORROW WILL ALWAYS BECOME A TODAY.

613. TODAY IS THE FIRST DAY OF THE REST OF YOUR LIFE.

614. TODAY IS THE TOMORROW THAT YOU WORRIED ABOUT YESTERDAY.

615. WHEN WE DWELL ON THE PROBLEM, THE PROBLEM GETS BIGGER AND WHEN WE DWELL ON THE SOLUTION, THE SOLUTION GETS BIGGER.

616. THE THINGS THAT WE HAVE IN COMMON ARE MORE IMPORTANT THAN OUR DIFFERENCES.

617. TROUBLE IS A PART OF OUR LIFE, AND IF WE DON'T SHARE IT WE DON'T GIVE THE PERSON WHO LOVES US ENOUGH OF A CHANCE TO LOVE US ENOUGH.

618. WORRY IS LIKE A ROCKING HORSE, IT KEEPS YOU MOVING BUT NEVER LETS YOU GET ANYWHERE.

619. THE WORST THINGS THAT I'VE LIVED THROUGH NEVER HAPPENED.

620. IF YOU WANT TO BE ABLE TO TRUST OTHERS, TRY BECOMING TRUSTWORTHIER YOURSELF.

621. THE TRUTH WILL SET YOU FREE, BUT FIRST IT WILL PISS YOU OFF.

622. WHEN YOU FEEL YOUR WORST, TRY YOUR HARDEST.

623. THE TWELVE STEPS ARE BUT SUGGESTIONS AND SO IS PULLING THE RIP CORD ON A PARACHUTE.

624. THE THINGS THAT I AM GRATEFUL FOR TODAY, I WILL TAKE FOR GRANTED TOMORROW.

625. TODAY I HAVE A CHOICE: GOD'S WILL OR MINE.

626. SUCCESS AND FAILURE SHARE A COMMON DENOMINATOR – BOTH ARE TEMPORARY.

627. THE STEPS KEEP US FROM SUICIDE AND THE TRADITIONS KEEP US FROM HOMICIDE.

628. THE ANSWER THAT YOU ARE SEEKING IS IN THE STEPS.

629. IF A NEWCOMER IS READY FOR RECOVERY, YOU CAN'T SAY ANYTHING WRONG AND IF THE NEWCOMER IS NOT READY, YOU CAN'T SAY ANYTHING RIGHT.

630. I HAVE EVERYTHING THAT I NEED TO GET EVERYTHING THAT I NEED.

631. IF THE SUN COMES UP AND GOES DOWN, AND I DON'T PICK UP IN THE MIDDLE, THEN I'VE HAD A GOOD DAY.

632. TAKE CARE OF THE DAYS AND THE YEARS WILL COME BY THEMSELVES.

633. WE MUST GIVE AWAY WHAT WE CANNOT KEEP, SO THAT WE MIGHT RECEIVE WHAT WE CANNOT LOSE.

634. SHOW UP TO GROW UP.

635. BY RELEASING RESENTMENT, WE SET OURSELVES FREE.

636. IF I'M OKAY WITH ME, I DON'T HAVE TO MAKE YOU WRONG.

637. TO THINE OWN SELF BE TRUE.

638. THERE ARE ONLY TWO SINS IN RECOVERY: TO STAND IN THE WAY OF SOMEONE ELSE'S GROWTH OR TO STAND IN THE WAY OF YOUR OWN.

639. THE SLICKER, THE SICKER.

640. RECOVERY IS A GIFT, THE PRICE OF WHICH IS ETERNAL VIGILANCE.

641. WHAT I CAME TO THE ROOMS LOOKING FOR, I CAME LOOKING WITH.

642. THE STEPS ARE THERE TO PROTECT ME AGAINST MYSELF AND THE TRADITIONS ARE THERE TO PROTECT THE FELLOWSHIP FROM ME.

643. SUCCESS IS NOT ABOUT GETTING WHAT YOU WANT; IT'S KNOWING WHAT YOU DON'T NEED.

644. T.I.M.E.: THINGS I MUST EARN; THIS IS MY EDUCATION.

645. DO YOU TALK THE TALK OR WALK THE TALK?

646. WORRYING ABOUT TOMORROW SAPS TODAY OF ITS STRENGTH.

647. WE DRINK TO BE COMFORTABLE WITH BEING UNCOMFORTABLE.

648. THE VICTIMS OF ADDICTION ARE THOSE AROUND US.

649. TOMORROW IS A PROMISSORY NOTE, YESTERDAY IS A CANCELED CHECK, AND TODAY IS A REALITY CHECK.

650. TALKING ABOUT THE SPIRITUAL PART OF THE PROGRAM IS LIKE TALKING ABOUT THE WET PART OF THE OCEAN.

651. PICK UP THE "BASIC TEXT" BEFORE YOU PICK UP.

652. DO THE STEPS NOW TO GET BETTER AND DON'T WAIT TO GET BETTER TO DO THE STEPS.

653. SOME OF US GET SO SPIRITUAL THAT WE ARE OF NO EARTHLY VALUE TO ANYONE.

654. RECOVERY IS GOD'S GIFT TO ME AND WHAT I DO WITH IT IS MY GIFT TO GOD.

655. EACH TIME YOU COME BACK INTO RECOVERY THE TUITION GOES UP.

656. IF YOU ESCAPED THE LION'S DEN, WHY GO BACK FOR YOUR HAT.

657. IF YOU FAIL TO CHANGE THE PERSON YOU WERE WHEN YOU CAME INTO THE FELLOWSHIP, THAT PERSON WILL TAKE YOU BACK OUT.

658. IF YOU GO OUT YOUR BOTTOM WILL GET LOWER.

659. WHEN I TIGHTEN THE NOOSE OF RESENTMENT AROUND SOMEONE'S NECK I CHOKE MYSELF.

660. OUR FELLOWSHIP IS A SELF-HELP PROGRAM THAT YOU CAN'T DO BY YOURSELF.

661. WE DON'T GET PARTIAL RESULTS FROM HALF MEASURES.

662. IF YOU WANT TO BURY SOMEONE WITH REVENGE YOU'LL HAVE TO DIG TWO GRAVES.

663. ALL YOU HAVE TO DO TO CHANGE YOUR LIFE IS TO CHANGE YOUR MIND.

664. GOD DOESN'T NEED MUCH TO WORK WITH, SO WHATEVER YOU HAVE LEFT IS FINE.

665. PRAYER IS NOT A DEVICE FOR GETTING MY OWN WAY, BUT RATHER A MEANS TO BECOME WHAT I SHOULD BE.

666. WE DON'T PRAY TO CHANGE THINGS; WE PRAY TO CHANGE US AND THE WAY THAT WE THINK.

667. A.S.A.P.: ALWAYS SAY A PRAYER.

668. BEAUTY AND TRUTH ARE ADMIRED AND PAIN IS OBEYED.

669. NOT FACING PAIN CAN PROLONG IT.

670. IF YOU GO TO ENOUGH MEETINGS, AND YOU STILL CAN'T STOP DRINKING, YOUR DRINKING WILL BE RUINED.

671. IF YOUR NOT GETTING MAD DURING SOME MEETINGS, YOU'RE PROBABLY NOT GOING TO ENOUGH MEETINGS.

672. LIVE IN THE MOMENT AND LIVE IN THE SOLUTION.

673. BEFORE WE CAME INTO THE FELLOWSHIP WE TREATED LONELINESS WITH ISOLATION.

674. JUST WHEN YOU THINK THAT YOU HAVE HUMILITY, YOU MAY HAVE LOST IT.

675. IDENTIFY AND DON'T COMPARE.

676. INSANITY IS DOING THE SAME THING OVER AND OVER AGAIN AND EXPECTING A DIFFERENT RESULT.

677. KEEP THE BEFORE-RECOVERY MEMORY GREEN.

678. IF YOU AREN'T HAPPY TODAY, THEN WHAT ARE YOU WAITING FOR?

679. IT IS EASIER TO LIVE YOUR WAY INTO GOOD FEELING THAN TO FEEL YOUR WAY INTO GOOD LIVING.

680. THERE IS NOTHING THAT WE CAN DO TO MAKE GOD LOVE US MORE THAN GOD ALREADY DOES AND THERE IS NOTHING WE CAN DO WRONG THAT WILL MAKE GOD LOVE US ANY LESS.

681. THE GRACE OF GOD WILL NEVER TAKE ME WHERE THE GRACE OF GOD WILL NOT PROTECT ME.

682. YOU CAN'T DO YOUR HIGHER POWER'S WILL YOUR WAY.

683. IF YOU WANT TO MAKE GOD LAUGH, TELL HIM YOUR PLANS FOR THE DAY.

684. FAITH IS HOPE IN THINGS UNSEEN.

685. FAITH WAS THE FIRST MEDICINE KNOWN TO MAN.

686. THE PERSON TAKES A DRINK, THE DRINK TAKES A DRINK, AND THEN THE DRINK TAKES THE PERSON.

687. DRINKING DIDN'T DROWN MY PROBLEMS, IT IRRIGATED THEM.

688. FEAR IS HEALTHY, BUT IT HAS NO POWER UNLESS I GIVE IT POWER.

689. FEAR IS WHAT KEEPS YOU FROM GOD'S PLAN FOR YOU.

690. I KNOW THAT GOD WILL NOT GIVE ME ANYTHING THAT I CAN'T HANDLE.

691. IF YOU DON'T THINK THAT THE FELLOWSHIP WILL HELP YOU, TRY IT AND IF YOU DON'T THINK THAT GOD WILL HELP YOU, ASK HIM.

692. A HISTORY OF MY DRINKING CAREER:
I DRANK TO STIMULATE THOUGHT AND BLACKED OUT;
I DRANK TO MAKE CONVERSATION AND TIED MY TONGUE;
I DRANK TO "CHILL" AND LOST MY COOL;
I DRANK FOR WARMTH AND LOST MY PLACE OF RESIDENCE;
I DRANK TO FORGET AND BECAME HAUNTED;
I DRANK FOR FREEDOM AND BECAME A SLAVE;
I DRANK FOR POWER AND BECAME POWERLESS;
I DRANK TO ERASE MY PROBLEMS AND SAW THEM

MULTIPLY;
I DRANK TO COPE WITH LIFE AND INVITED DEATH . . .
OR WORSE;
I DRANK BECAUSE I HAD A RIGHT AND EVERYTHING
TURNED OUT WRONG.

AUTHOR UNKNOWN

693. A FREE DRINK IS OFTEN THE MOST EXPENSIVE.

694. THERE, BUT FOR THE GRACE OF GOD, GO I.

695. GRATEFUL ADDICTS DON'T USE AND USING ADDICTS ARE NOT GRATEFUL.

696. IF YOUR HEART IS FULL OF GRATITUDE, THERE IS NO ROOM FOR RESENTMENT.

697. KEEP AN ATTITUDE OF GRATITUDE.

698. SHOW UP AND GROW UP.

699. DON'T COMMIT SUICIDE DURING YOUR FIRST FIVE YEARS IN RECOVERY BECAUSE YOU'LL BE KILLING THE WRONG PERSON.

700. IF SMALL THINGS MAKE YOU ANGRY, THEN JUST HOW BIG ARE YOU?

701. MOST FOLKS ARE AS HAPPY AS THEY MAKE UP THEIR MINDS TO BE.

702. ASKING FOR HELP IS NOT A BAD THING.

703. H.O.P.E.: HANG ON, PEACE EXISTS.

704. KIND IS BETTER THAN RIGHT.

705. INSANITY IS THE SEEMINGLY INABILITY TO LEARN FROM PAST MISTAKES.

706. THE TROUBLE WITH STAYING HOME AND ISOLATING IS THAT YOU GET A LOT OF BAD ADVICE.

707. IF YOU CAN'T TAKE IT LEAVE IT AND IF YOU CAN'T LEAVE IT, THEN LOVE IT.

708. GOD ONLY LENDS US PEOPLE WHEN WE NEED THEM.

709. IT ISN'T "ME" AND "YOU" ANYMORE, IT'S "WE" AND "US."

710. IF YOU BRING YOUR BODY, YOUR MIND WILL FOLLOW.

711. MEETINGS ARE NOT ENOUGH.

712. PEOPLE WHO DON'T GO MEETINGS DON'T FIND OUT WHAT HAPPENS TO PEOPLE WHO DON'T GO TO MEETINGS.

713. NEGATIVITY IS MY DISEASE TELLING ME TO COME OUT AND PLAY.

714. WHAT COMES AFTER 90 DAYS?   91, 92, 93, ETC.!

715. SOME OF US GO TO MEETINGS FOR ALL SORTS OF REASONS, BUT WE DON'T KNOW WHAT THEY ARE, SO WE KEEP GOING TO MEETINGS!

716. IF LOVE HAS CONDITIONS ATTACHED, THEN IT'S NOT LOVE - IT'S BARTER.

717. LOVE IS A VERB, WHICH IS DEFINED AS AN ACTION.

718. LOVE ISN'T LOVE UNTIL YOU GIVE IT AWAY.

719. MEETINGS ARE LIKE SOME RAFFLES; YOU MUST BE PRESENT TO WIN.

720. SUIT UP, SHOW UP, SHUT UP, AND GROW UP.

721. THOSE WHO GET AROUND WILL STAY AROUND.

722. IF YOU START TO SKIP, THEN YOU'LL START TO SLIP.

723. A MEETING A DAY KEEPS THE DETOX AWAY.

724. BEING HUMBLE MEANS BEING TEACHABLE.

725. GET HUMBLE OR BE MADE HUMBLE!

726. IT'S NOT SO IMPORTANT AS TO WHY YOU ARE AN ADDICT, BUT RATHER WHAT YOU INTEND TO DO ABOUT IT.

727. PAIN IS MANDATORY, BUT SUFFERING IS OPTIONAL!

728. THE OPPOSITE OF JOY IS NOT SORROW - IT'S CYNICISM.

729. WHEN THE PAIN OF WHERE I AM IS WORSE THAN THE DISCOMFORT OF WHERE I AM GOING, THEN I'LL MOVE.

730. WHEN YOU FEEL THAT IT'S YOUR JOB TO HUMBLE OTHERS, YOU MAY BE IN FOR A STUMBLE, A FUMBLE, OR A CRUMBLE.

731. HUMILITY IS LIKE A VENEREAL DISEASE BECAUSE IF YOU HAVE IT YOU DON'T WANT TO TALK ABOUT IT.

732. HALOS CAN TURN INTO NOOSES.

733. WHEN YOU ARE IN A MEETING, YOUR DISEASE IS OUTSIDE DOING PUSH-UPS.

734. YOU ONLY HAVE TO GO TO MEETINGS UNTIL YOU WANT TO GO.

735. FOCUS + COURAGE + WILLINGNESS TO LEARN = MIRACLES!

736. THE ONLY AVOIDABLE PAIN IS THE PAIN WE ENDURE IN THE PROCESS OF TRYING TO AVOID THE PAIN.

737. GOD, GRANT ME PATIENCE . . . NOW!

738. PLAN PLANS, NOT RESULTS.

739. YOU CAN'T GET INDIGESTION FROM SWALLOWING YOUR PRIDE.

740. I WAS NOT A "PROBLEM DRINKER," BUT EVERY TIME I DRANK I HAD A PROBLEM!

741. DON'T WORRY IF YOU DON'T GET THE PROGRAM RIGHT AWAY, BECAUSE IT WILL GET YOU!

742. THE PROGRAM IS LIKE A SUBMARINE BECAUSE IT IS MUCH BETTER TO BE IN IT THAN AROUND IT.

743. TAKE THE PROGRAM SERIOUSLY, NOT YOURSELF.

744. I KNOW THAT I'M GETTING BETTER BECAUSE I SAVE MY BEST ARGUMENT FOR WHEN SOMEONE ELSE IS IN THE ROOM.

745. DISCOVER YOURSELF BECAUSE EVERYTHING ELSE HAS BEEN DONE TO FORM THE PROGRAM.

746. WE TAKE THE STEPS, BUT IT'S FUNNY WHERE THE STEPS TAKE US.

747. MAY YOU BE BLESSED WITH A SLOW RECOVERY.

748. R.E.L.A.P.S.E.: RELIVING EVERY LOW AND PITIFUL SCENE EXACTLY.

749. REHABS ARE FOR QUITTERS.

750. FOR TRUE INTIMACY TO TAKE PLACE, I MUST BE A WHOLE PERSON FORMING A PARTNERSHIP AND NOT A BROKEN PERSON SEEKING ANOTHER TO BE WHOLE.

751. IF YOU CAN ACCEPT THAT EVERY THING IS AS IT SHOULD BE THEN YOU ARE SERENE.

752. SHUT UP, SHOW UP, AND SAY, "YES" TO SERVICE WORK.

753. TRUST IN GOD, CLEAN HOUSE, AND WORK WITH OTHERS.

754. BE A CHANNEL AND NOT A DAM.

755. GIVE TO GOD AND GOD WILL GIVE TO YOU.

756. NO ONE HAS EVER TRIPPED OVER A MOUNTAIN, BUT SOME CAN SURE TRIP OVER A PEBBLE AND FALL.

757. S.L.I.P.: SERENITY LOOSES ITS PRIORITY;
SOMETHING LOUSY I PLANNED; STUPID
LITTLE IDIOTIC PLAN.

758. WHEN YOU DANCE WITH A GORILLA, IT'S THE
GORILLA WHO DECIDES WHEN YOU STOP.

759. MOST PEOPLE TRY TO AVOID HELL, WHILE SPIRITUAL
PEOPLE HAVE BEEN THERE.

760. GOD GAVE US A KIT OF SPIRITUAL TOOLS, BUT IT'S
UP TO US TO USE THEM TO BUILD A DURABLE
SHELTER.

761. IF YOU HAVE A PROBLEM BELIEVING IN GOD THEN
GO TO A MEETING AND SEE MIRACLE, AFTER
MIRACLE, AFTER MIRACLE: SEEING IS BELIEVING.

762. I GET WHAT I NEED AND INEVITABLY FIND OUT
THAT IT WAS WHAT I WANTED ALL THE TIME.

763. LIFE IS A DANCE WHEN YOU LEARN THE STEPS.

764. SOMETIMES YOU HAVE TO STOP LOOKING TO FIND
WHAT YOU NEED.

765. WORK THE PROGRAM AND NOT THE PROBLEM.

766. PROGRESS NOT PERFECTION.

767. WE CAME (DRINKIE), WE SAW (DRANKIE),
WE CONQUERED (DRUNKIE).

768. IF YOU WANT TO FEEL BETTER RIGHT AWAY, THEN
ASK GOD TO HELP YOU BE OF SERVICE.

769. IF THE MILLIONS OF PEOPLE IN RECOVERY ARE
WRONG, THEN I'M SCREWED.

770. YESTERDAY IS HISTORY, TOMORROW IS A MYSTERY,
AND TODAY IS A GIFT FROM MY HIGHER POWER....
THAT'S WHY I CALL IT THE PRESENT.

771. ALCOHOL TOOK EVERYTHING AWAY FROM ME
BUT MY ABILITY TO BREATHE.

772. THE ONLY PROBLEMS THAT I HAVE TODAY IS
WHEN I BREAK OUT IN A RASH OF SELF-WILL.

773. SINCE I'VE JOINED THE FELLOWSHIP I DON'T HAVE
ANY MORE PROBLEMS - JUST A FEW ISSUES OR
SITUATIONS ONCE IN A WHILE.

774. THAT PERSON THAT I ALWAYS SEE IN MY BATHROOM
MIRROR IS MY BEST FRIEND.

775. ARE YOU WILLING TO GIVE UP EVERYTHING THAT
YOU HAVE TO GET EVERYTHING THAT YOU NEED?

776. THE WAR IS OVER AND I LOST!

777. WHEN GOD GAVE ME A BIRTHDAY HE ALSO GAVE
ME A DEATH DAY.

778. MY ANSWERING MACHINE WILL TELL YOU HOW
I'M DOING TODAY: "I APOLOGIZE FOR NOT BEING
HERE TO ANSWER YOUR CALL. I'VE PROBABLY
GONE SOMEWHERE I'VE NEVER BEEN BEFORE,
TO MEET SOME FRIENDS THAT I'VE NEVER MET
BEFORE, TO TALK ABOUT THE THINGS THAT I DON'T
DO ANYMORE"

779. WE WILL ATTAIN AND MAINTAIN RECOVERY.

780. "WE ARE GOING TO KNOW A NEW FREEDOM AND
A NEW HAPPINESS.

781. WE WILL NOT REGRET THE PAST NOR WISH TO
SHUT THE DOOR ON IT.

782. WE WILL COMPREHEND THE WORD SERENITY AND
WE WILL KNOW PEACE.

783. NO MATTER HOW FAR DOWN THE SCALE WE HAVE
GONE, WE WILL SEE HOW OUR EXPERIENCES CAN
BENEFIT OTHERS.

784. THAT FEELING OF USELESSNESS AND SELF-PITY
WILL DISAPPEAR.

785. WE WILL LOSE INTEREST IN SELFISH THINGS AND GAIN INTEREST IN OUR FELLOWS.

786. SELF-SEEKING WILL SLIP AWAY.

787. OUR WHOLE ATTITUDE AND OUTLOOK UPON LIFE WILL CHANGE.

788. FEAR OF PEOPLE AND ECONOMIC INSECURITY WILL LEAVE US.

789. WE WILL INTUITIVELY KNOW HOW TO HANDLE SITUATIONS WHICH USE TO BAFFLE US.

790. WE WILL SUDDENLY REALIZE THAT GOD IS DOING FOR US WHAT WE COULD NOT DO FOR OURSELVES."
ALCOHOLICS ANONYMOUS, THIRD EDITION
PAGES 83-84

791. LEARN TO FOLLOW YOUR HIGHER POWER'S WILL FOR YOURSELF AND YOU WILL PRESENTLY LIVE IN A NEW AND WONDERFUL WORLD, NO MATTER WHAT YOUR PRESENT CIRCUMSTANCES!

792. CLEAN AND SERENE OR CLEAN AND CRAZY.

793. PURE ALCOHOLIC DEFINED: A MAMMAL GOING INTO EXTINCTION.

794. THE HARDEST JOURNEY OUR RECOVERY CAN EVER MAKE IS GOING FROM OUR HEADS TO OUR HEARTS.

795. WHEN YOUR CIRCLE OF FRIENDS STOPS GROWING, YOU STOP GROWING.

796. HANGING OUT IN MY HEAD IS LIKE LIVING IN A HAUNTED HOUSE.

797. UNITED WE STAND, DIVIDED WE FALL.

798. MY HEAD IS LIKE A BAD NEIGHBORHOOD AND I'M NOT ALLOWED TO GO THERE ALONE.

799. BEFORE I CAME INTO RECOVERY, I WAS A CARD
CARRYING MEMBER OF THE "OUT-TO-LUNCH
BUNCH."

800. DO YOU LOVE YOURSELF ENOUGH TO GIVE
YOURSELF A BREAK?

801. MY DEGREE OF ACCEPTANCE IS CONTROLLED
BY MY SELECTIVE HEARING.

802. THERE ARE THREE WAYS OF DOING SOMETHING:
THE RIGHT WAY, THE WRONG WAY, AND THE WAY
THAT SOMEONE ELSE WANTS IT DONE.

803. ARE YOU WORKING A RECOVERY PROGRAM OR
A REVOLVING DOOR PROGRAM?

804. IN ORDER TO STAY IN RECOVERY, I HAVE TO
INSPECT THE PATIENCE, WILLINGNESS, HONESTY,
AND OPEN-MINDEDNESS OF MY FOUNDATION
EACH AND EVERY MORNING.

805. SERENITY COMES ONLY FROM WORKING THE
STEPS, IN ORDER, ONE AT A TIME.

806. IF WE GIVE IN TO OUR RELUCTANCE TO REVEAL
THE TRUE NATURE OF WHO WE ARE, TO EVEN
ONE HUMAN BEING, THE SECRET SIDE OF OUR
LIVES BECOMES EVEN MORE POWERFUL.

807. A SIMPLE, HONEST MESSAGE OF RECOVERY
ALWAYS RINGS TRUE.

808. THE STEPS LEAD TO AN AWAKENING OF A
SPIRITUAL NATURE WITHIN US AND THIS
AWAKENING IS EVIDENCED BY CHANGES IN OUR
LIVES THAT OTHERS SEE.

809. THE DIFFERENCE BETWEEN BEING ALONE AND
BEING LONELY IS THAT BEING ALONE IS A STATE
OF THE HEART AND BEING LONELY IS NOT ALWAYS
ALLEVIATED WHEN WE ENTER INTO RELATIONSHIPS.

810. THE MAN IN THE GLASS:
WHEN YOU GET WHAT YOU WANT IN YOUR STRUGGLE

FOR SELFAND THE WORLD MAKES YOU KING FOR A DAY, JUST GO TO A MIRROR AND LOOK AT YOURSELF AND SEE WHAT THAT MAN HAS TO SAY. FOR IT ISN'T YOUR FATHER OR MOTHER OR WIFE WHOSE JUDGMENT UPON YOU MUST PASS, THE FELLOW WHOSE VERDICT COUNTS MOST IN YOUR LIFE IS THE ONE STARING BACK FROM THE GLASS. SOME PEOPLE MAY THINK YOU A STRAIGHT-SHOOTIN' CHUM AND CALL YOU A WONDERFUL GUY, BUT THE MAN IN THE GLASS SAYS YOU'RE ONLY A BUM IF YOU CAN'T LOOK HIM STRAIGHT IN THE EYE. HE'S THE FELLOW TO PLEASE, NEVER MIND ALL THE REST FOR HE'S WITH YOU CLEAR UP TO THE END. AND YOU'VE PASSED YOUR MOST DANGEROUS, DIFFICULT TEST IF THE MAN IN THE GLASS IS YOUR FRIEND. YOU MAY FOOL THE WHOLE WORLD DOWN THE PATHWAY OF LIFE AND GET PATS ON YOUR BACK AS YOU PASS, BUT YOUR FINAL REWARD WILL BE HEARTACHES AND TEARS IF YOU'VE CHEATED THE MAN IN THE GLASS.

M. SMITH   1912

811.   THE SERENITY PRAYER:
GOD GRANT ME THE SERENITY TO ACCEPT THE THINGS I CANNOT CHANGE; COURAGE TO CHANGE THE THINGS I CAN; AND WISDOM TO KNOW THE DIFFERENCE - LIVING ONE DAY AT A TIME; ENJOYING ONE MOMENT AT A TIME; ACCEPTING HARDSHIPS AS THE PATHWAY TO PEACE; TAKING, AS HE DID, THIS SINFUL WORLD AS IT IS, NOT AS I WOULD HAVE IT; TRUSTING THAT HE WILL MAKE ALL THINGS RIGHT IF I SURRENDER TO HIS WILL; THAT I MAY BE REASONABLY HAPPY IN THIS LIFE AND SUPREMELY HAPPY WITH HIM FOREVER IN THE NEXT.

REVEREND REINHOLD NIEBUHR   1943
UNION THEOLOGICAL SEMINARY
NEW YORK, NEW YORK

812.   I AM ADDICTION:
I AM MORE POWERFUL THAN THE COMBINED ARMIES OF THE WORLD. I HAVE DESTROYED MORE MEN AND WOMEN THAN ALL OF THE WARS OF THE WORLD. I HAVE CAUSED MILLIONS UPON MILLIONS OF ACCIDENTS AND WRECKED MORE HOMES THAN ALL OF THE FLOODS, TORNADOES, AND HURRICANES OF THE WORLD PUT TOGETHER. I AM THE WORLD'S

SLICKEST THIEF IN THAT I STEAL COUNTLESS
DOLLARS EACH AND EVERY YEAR. I FIND MY VICTIMS
AMONG THE RICH, POOR, YOUNG, OLD, STRONG,
WEAK, EDUCATED, AND ILLITERATE BECAUSE I DO
NOT DISCRIMINATE. I LOOM UP TO SUCH
PROPORTIONS THAT I CAST A SHADOW OVER EVERY
SQUARE INCH OF THIS WORLD. I AM RELENTLESS,
INSIDIOUS, AND UNPREDICTABLE. I AM EVERYWHERE:
IN THE HOME; ON THE STREET; IN THE FACTORY; IN
THE OFFICE; ON THE SEA AND; IN THE AIR. I AM
SICKNESS, POVERTY, AND DEATH. I GIVE NOTHING
AND TAKE ALL. I AM YOUR WORST NIGHTMARE. I AM
ADDICTION.

AUTHOR UNKNOWN

813. IF I TRY TO RAISE MY BOTTOM, AS I MOVE ALONG
      IN MY RECOVERY, I MAY BE SETTING MYSELF UP
      FOR ANOTHER RUN.

814. WE PROGRESS AND MATURE THROUGH FAULTS.

815. IF FAITH WITHOUT WORKS IS DEAD, THEN
      WILLINGNESS WITHOUT ACTION IS FANTASY.

816. A.C.T.I.O.N.: ANY CHANGE THAT IMPROVES
      ONE'S NATURE.

817. YOU DON'T HAVE TO BE A SQUIRREL TO GO OUT
      ON A LIMB AND GAIN THE FRUIT OF YOUR LABOR.

818. IT IS WHAT IT IS BECAUSE THAT'S WHAT IT IS.

819. KEEP COMING BACK . . . . BETTER YET, STAY!

820. "THE SIX CHUNKS OF TRUTH" (THE ORIGINAL
      STEPS TO RECOVERY):
      1. WE ADMITTED THAT WE WERE LICKED, THAT WE
         WERE POWERLESS OVER ALCOHOL.
      2. WE MADE A MORAL INVENTORY OF OUR DEFECTS OR SINS.
      3. WE CONFESSED OR SHARED OUR SHORTCOMINGS
         WITH ANOTHER PERSON IN CONFIDENCE.
      4. WE MADE RESTITUTION TO ALL THOSE WE HAD
         HARMED BY OUR DRINKING.
      5. WE TRIED TO HELP OTHER ALCOHOLICS, WITH NO
         THOUGHT OF REWARD IN MONEY OR PRESTIGE.

6. WE PRAYED TO WHATEVER GOD WE THOUGHT
THERE WAS FOR POWER TO PRACTICE THESE
PRECEPTS.

PASS IT ON, PAGE 197

821. THE FIVE "C'S":
1. CONFIDENCE.
2. CONFESSION.
3. CONVICTION.
4. CONVERSION.
5. CONTINUANCE.

DR. BOB AND THE GOOD OLD TIMERS, PAGE 54

822. THE FIVE PROCEDURES:
1. GIVE IN TO GOD.
2. LISTEN TO GOD'S DIRECTION.
3. CHECK GUIDANCE.
4. RESTITUTION.
5. SHARING.

DR. BOB AND THE GOOD OLD TIMERS, PAGES 54 – 55

823. THE FOUR ABSOLUTES:
1. ABSOLUTE HONESTY.
2. ABSOLUTE UNSELFISHNESS.
3. ABSOLUTE PURITY.
4. ABSOLUTE LOVE.

DR. BOB AND THE GOOD OLD TIMERS, PAGE 54

824. DEAR LORD:
SO FAR TODAY, GOD, I'VE DONE ALL RIGHT. I
HAVEN'T GOSSIPED, HAVEN'T LOST MY TEMPER,
HAVEN'T BEEN GREEDY, GRUMPY, NASTY, SELFISH,
OR OVER-INDULGENT. I'M THANKFUL FOR THAT.
BUT, IN A FEW MINUTES, GOD, I'M GOING TO GET OUT
OF BED AND FROM THEN ON I'M PROBABLY GOING TO
NEED A LOT MORE HELP. AMEN.

AUTHOR UNKNOWN

825. IF YOU DON'T STAND FOR SOMETHING, YOU'LL
FALL FOR ANYTHING.

826. ACCEPTANCE IS THE MASTER KEY TO ALL OF THE
SITUATIONS THAT I FACE.

827. O.P.P.S.: OFTEN PROCRASTINATING PERFORMING STEPS.

828. WHY THE STEPS WORK:
STEP 1   A STATEMENT OF THE PROBLEM.
STEP 2   A STATEMENT OF THE SOLUTION.
STEPS 3 THRU 12   HOW TO ARRIVE AT THE SOLUTION.

829. IF YOU'RE PLANNING A "PITY PARTY," DON'T FORGET TO INVITE YOUR SPONSOR, YOUR HOME GROUP, AND TO BRING THE REFRESHMENTS!

830. THE ROOMS OF RECOVERY CONTAIN A TEACHING PROGRAM, NOT A PREACHING PROGRAM.

831. I CAN'T IMPRESS SOMEONE WITH THE AMOUNT OF TIME THAT I HAVE IN RECOVERY, BUT PERHAPS I WILL WITH THE SPIRITUAL CONTENT OF THAT RECOVERY.

832. FOOTPRINTS:
ONE NIGHT A MAN HAD A DREAM. HE DREAMED HE WAS WALKING ALONG THE BEACH WITH THE LORD. ACROSS THE SKY FLASHED SCENES FROM HIS LIFE. FOR EACH SCENE, HE NOTICED TWO SETS OF FOOTPRINTS IN THE SAND, ONE BELONGING TO HIM, AND THE OTHER TO THE LORD. WHEN THE LAST SCENE OF HIS LIFE FLASHED BEFORE HIM, HE LOOKED BACK AT THE FOOTPRINTS IN THE SAND. HE NOTICED THAT MANY TIMES ALONG THE PATH OF HIS LIFE THERE WAS ONLY ONE SET OF FOOTPRINTS. HE ALSO NOTICED THAT IT HAPPENED AT THE VERY LOWEST AND SADDEST TIMES OF HIS LIFE. THIS REALLY BOTHERED HIM AND HE QUESTIONED THE LORD ABOUT IT. "LORD, YOU SAID THAT ONCE I DECIDED TO FOLLOW YOU, YOU'D WALK WITH ME ALL THE WAY. BUT I HAVE NOTICED THAT DURING THE MOST TROUBLESOME TIMES IN MY LIFE, THERE IS ONLY ONE SET OF FOOTPRINTS. I DON'T UNDERSTAND WHY WHEN I NEEDED YOU MOST YOU WOULD LEAVE ME." THE LORD REPLIED, "MY PRECIOUS, PRECIOUS CHILD, I LOVE YOU AND I WOULD NEVER LEAVE YOU. DURING YOUR TIMES OF TRIAL AND SUFFERING, WHEN YOU SEE ONLY ONE SET OF FOOTPRINTS, IT WAS THEN THAT I CARRIED YOU."

                                        AUTHOR UNKNOWN

THE NEXT NIGHT THE MAN HAD ANOTHER DREAM. HE
AGAIN DREAMED THAT HE WAS WALKING ALONG THE
BEACH WITH THE LORD. AS THE SKY FLASHED THE
SCENES OF HIS LIFE, HE SMILED AS HE SAW THE TWO
SETS AND ONE SET OF FOOTPRINTS IN THE SAND
APPEAR AGAIN AND AGAIN. AFTER HE WATCHED THE
LAST SCENE, AND LOOKED BACK OVER THE
FOOTPRINTS IN THE SAND, HIS EYES CAME TO REST AT
WHERE HE STOOD. SURROUNDING HIM WERE TWO
SETS OF FOOTPRINTS GOING THIS WAY AND THAT
WAY IN THE SAND AROUND HIM. AT THAT MOMENT,
HE FELT A JOY AND PEACE WITHIN HIMSELF THAT HE
HAD NEVER EXPERIENCED BEFORE. FOR HE KNEW
THAT HE WAS DANCING WITH THE LORD.

AUTHOR UNKNOWN

833. THE SMALLEST RECOVERY MEETING IN THE
WORLD CONSISTS OF GOD, THE "BASIC TEXT,"
AND AN INDIVIDUAL WHO WANTS RECOVERY.

834. THE ROOMS OF RECOVERY WILL EXIST, THROUGH
THE GRACE OF GOD, FOR AS LONG AS HE SHALL
NEED US.

835. PRACTICE PREVENTIVE MEDICINE BY CHANGING
PEOPLE, PLACES, AND THINGS.

836. IF USING IS THE ANSWER, THEN WHAT IS THE
QUESTION?

837. THE FELLOWSHIP IS THE BIGGEST AND GREATEST
LOST AND FOUND DEPARTMENT IN THE WORLD.

838. THE PUZZLE:
ONE MORNING, A MAN APPROACHED HIS 14 YEAR OLD
SON AND ASKED HIM, "SON, WHY ARE YOU FAILING
YOUR STUDIES IN YOUR GEOGRAPHY CLASS?" THE
SON'S REPLY WAS, "I DON'T KNOW, FATHER." BEING A
PATIENT AND LOVING FATHER, THE MAN DECIDED TO
GENTLY GUIDE HIS SON THROUGH THE SITUATION. HE
PURCHASED A 10" X 14" MAP OF THE WORLD AND
GLUED IT UPON AN OLD POSTERBOARD OF THE SAME
SIZE THAT THE STORE OWNER GAVE TO HIM .
CAREFULLY, HE CUT EACH COUNTRY OUT OF THE

MAP, SEPARATING THE OCEANS ALONG THE LATITUDE
AND LONGITUDE LINES, AND PLACED THE PIECES IN A
BOX. THAT AFTERNOON, HE PRESENTED THE BOX TO
HIS CHILD SAYING, "SON, IF YOU WILL PUT THIS
PUZZLE TOGETHER FOR ME WE WILL BE ABLE TO GO
TO THE BASEBALL GAME TOGETHER TONIGHT."
AFTER A COUPLE OF HOURS HAD PASSED, THE SON
CAME TO HIS FATHER AND SAID, "FATHER, I HAVE
COMPLETED THE PUZZLE." "HOW DID YOU FINISH SO
QUICKLY?" SAID THE FATHER. WITH A SMILE, THE
SON REPLIED, "THERE WAS A PICTURE OF A MAN ON
THE BACK. WHEN I PUT THE MAN TOGETHER, THE
WORLD FELL INTO PLACE."

AUTHOR UNKNOWN

839. GARBAGE IN, GARBAGE OUT.

840. IN RECOVERY, WE GET INTO THE THANK YOU
LINE AND NOT THE GIVE ME LINE.

841. ALCOHOL:
ALCOHOL IS A PRODUCT OF AMAZING VERSATILITY.
IT WILL REMOVE STAINS FROM DESIGNER CLOTHES.
IT WILL ALSO REMOVE CLOTHES OFF OF YOUR BACK.
IF BY CHANCE IT IS USED IN SUFFICIENT QUANTITY,
ALCOHOL WILL REMOVE FURNITURE FROM THE
HOME, RUGS FROM THE FLOOR, FOOD FROM THE
TABLE, LINING FROM THE STOMACH, VISION FROM
THE EYES, AND JUDGMENT FROM THE MIND.
ALCOHOL WILL ALSO REMOVE GOOD REPUTATIONS,
GOOD JOBS, GOOD FRIENDS, HAPPINESS FROM
CHILDREN'S HEARTS, SANITY, FREEDOM, SPOUSES,
RELATIONSHIPS, MAN'S ABILITY TO ADJUST AND LIVE
WITH HIS FELLOW MAN, AND EVEN LIFE ITSELF. AS A
REMOVER OF THINGS, ALCOHOL HAS NO EQUAL.

AUTHOR UNKNOWN

842. I AM YOUR DISEASE - ADDICTION:
I HATE MEETINGS. I HATE HIGHER POWER. I HATE
ANYONE WHO HAS A LIFE THAT INVOLVES A TWELVE-
STEP PROGRAM. I HATE SPONSORS. I HATE HOME
GROUPS. I WISH YOU DEATH AND I WISH YOU
SUFFERING. ALLOW ME TO INTRODUCE MYSELF - I AM
THE DISEASE OF ADDICTION! INSIDIOUS, CUNNING,
BAFFLING, AND POWERFUL ARE A FEW OF MY OTHER

NAMES. THAT'S ALL ME AND MORE. I HAVE KILLED MILLIONS AND I AM PLEASED WITH MY WORK. I LOVE TO CATCH YOU WITH THE ELEMENT OF SURPRISE. I LOVE TO PRETEND THAT I AM YOUR FRIEND AND LOVER. I HAVE GIVEN YOU COMFORT WHEN YOU NEEDED IT, HAVEN'T I? WASN'T I THERE WHEN YOU WERE LONELY? WHEN YOU WANTED TO DIE, DIDN'T YOU CALL UPON ME? I WAS THERE FOR YOU EVERY TIME. I LOVE TO MAKE YOU HURT. I LOVE TO MAKE YOU CRY. BETTER YET, I LOVE WHEN YOU ARE SO NUMB THAT YOU CAN NEITHER HURT NOR CRY. THAT IS WHEN YOU CAN'T FEEL ANYTHING AT ALL. THIS IS TRUE GLORY TO ME. I WILL GIVE YOU INSTANT GRATIFICATION AND ALL THAT I ASK OF YOU IS FOR A COMMITMENT TO LONG-TERM SUFFERING. I'VE BEEN THERE FOR YOU ALWAYS. WHEN THINGS WERE GOING RIGHT FOR YOU IN YOUR LIFE, YOU INVITED ME INTO YOUR LIFE. YOU SAID THAT YOU DIDN'T DESERVE THESE GOOD THINGS, AND I WAS THE ONLY ONE WHO WOULD AGREE WITH YOU. TOGETHER WE ARE ABLE TO DESTROY ALL GOOD IN YOUR LIFE. I AM SUCH A HATED DISEASE, AND YET I DO NOT COME INTO YOUR LIFE UNINVITED. YOU CHOOSE TO HAVE ME. YET, I AM NEVER ALONE IF YOU DON'T CALL FOR ME. MANY HAVE CHOSEN TO HAVE ME IN THEIR LIVES OVER REALITY AND PEACE. YET, MORE THAN YOU CAN HATE ME, I HATE ALL WHO WEAKEN ME WHEN I CAN'T FUNCTION IN THE MANNER THAT I AM ACCUSTOMED TO. WHEN THAT HAPPENS, I MUST WAIT HERE QUIETLY. YOU CAN'T SEE ME, BUT I AM GROWING AND GETTING STRONGER. BIGGER THEN EVER. WHEN YOU ONLY EXIST, I KEEP ON LIVING. WHEN YOU START TO LIVE, I ONLY EXIST. BUT, I AM HERE UNTIL WE MEET AGAIN, IF WE MEET AGAIN, AND I WISH YOU SUFFERING AND DEATH.

AUTHOR UNKNOWN

843.	THE TWELVE STEP RELAPSE PROGRAM:
1.	I DECIDED I COULD HANDLE ANY AND ALL EMOTIONAL PROBLEMS IF OTHER PEOPLE WOULD JUST QUIT TRYING TO RUN MY LIFE.
2.	I FIRMLY BELIEVE THAT THERE IS NO GREATER POWER THAN MYSELF AND ANYONE WHO SAYS DIFFERENTLY IS INSANE.
3.	I MADE A DECISION TO REMOVE MY WILL AND LIFE

FROM GOD, WHO DIDN'T UNDERSTAND ME ANYHOW.

4. I MADE A SEARCHING AND THOROUGH MORAL INVENTORY OF EVERYONE I KNOW, SO THEY COULDN'T FOOL ME AND TAKE ADVANTAGE OF MY GOOD NATURE.

5. I SOUGHT THESE PEOPLE OUT AND TRIED TO GET THEM TO ADMIT TO ME, BY GOD, THE NATURE OF THEIR WRONGS.

6. I BECAME WILLING TO HELP THESE PEOPLE GET RID OF THEIR DEFECTS OF CHARACTER.

7. I WAS HUMBLE ENOUGH TO ASK THESE PEOPLE TO REMOVE THEIR SHORTCOMINGS.

8. I KEPT A LIST OF ALL THE PEOPLE WHO HAD HARMED ME AND WAITED PATIENTLY FOR A CHANCE TO GET EVEN WITH THEM.

9. I GOT EVEN WITH THESE PEOPLE WHENEVER POSSIBLE, EXCEPT WHEN TO DO SO WOULD GET ME INTO TROUBLE.

10. I CONTINUE TO TAKE EVERYONE'S INVENTORY AND WHEN THEY ARE WRONG, WHICH IS MOST OF THE TIME, I PROMPTLY MAKE THEM ADMIT IT.

11. I SOUGHT THROUGH THE CONCENTRATION OF MY WILLPOWER TO GET GOD, WHO DIDN'T UNDERSTAND ME ANYHOW, TO SEE THAT MY IDEAS WERE BEST AND HE OUGHT TO GIVE ME THE POWER TO CARRY THEM OUT.

12. HAVING MAINTAINED MY EMOTIONAL PROBLEMS WITH THESE STEPS, I CAN THOROUGHLY RECOMMEND THEM TO OTHERS WHO DON'T WANT TO LOSE THEIR HARD EARNED STATUS, BUT WISH TO BE LEFT ALONE TO PRACTICE NEUROSIS IN EVERYTHING THEY DO FOR THE REST OF THEIR DAYS.

AUTHOR UNKNOWN

844. WHAT YOU DO SPEAKS SO LOUDLY THAT I CAN'T HEAR A WORD THAT YOU ARE SAYING.

845. THE WHISTLE ON THE TRAIN ISN'T WARNING YOU ABOUT THE SECOND CAR OF THE TRAIN.

846. THE DEVINE ORDER OF LIVING: GOD, SELF, AND OTHERS.

847. THERE ARE NO LOSERS IN RECOVERY, ONLY
SLOW WINNERS.

848. NEVER PUT A QUESTION MARK WHERE YOUR
HIGHER POWER PUTS A PERIOD.

849. TRYING TO FILL THAT HOLE IN YOUR GUT WITH
ANYTHING BUT A HIGHER POWER IS LIKE TRYING TO
SHOVEL SMOKE.

850. HIGHER POWER PROTECTION:
ONE EVENING, AROUND 7:30 P.M., I WAS ALONE AND
CROSSING THROUGH A LOCAL PARK ON MY WAY TO A
LATE MEETING WHEN I MET AN OLD FRIEND WHO WAS
STILL NOT IN THE ROOMS OF RECOVERY. WE
EXCHANGED GREETINGS, TALKED BRIEFLY ABOUT
"THE GOOD OL' DAYS," WHAT LIFE WAS LIKE TODAY,
AND THEN I WENT ON MY MERRY WAY. THAT NIGHT,
AS I WATCHED THE LATE NIGHT NEWS, I HEARD THAT
MY FRIEND HAD BEEN ARRESTED FOR SEVERAL
MURDERS WHICH HAD OCCURRED BETWEEN THE
HOURS OF 7 AND 10 P.M. THAT EVENING. THE NEXT
DAY I WENT TO VISIT MY FRIEND IN JAIL AND I ASKED
WHY I WAS ALLOWED TO LEAVE AND NOT COUNTED
AMONG THOSE THAT WERE KILLED. MY FRIEND SAID
THESE THREE WORDS AND LEFT: "YOU WEREN'T
ALONE!"   AUTHOR UNKNOWN

851. I AM AN EAGLE:
ONE DAY AN EAGLE WAS SOARING ALONE THROUGH
THE SKY WHEN HE SPOTTED A FLOCK OF BIRDS
SOARING, SIMILAR TO HIM, SOME DISTANCE AWAY.
WANTING COMPANY, HE DECIDED TO JOIN THEM. AS
HE APPROACHED, HE REALIZED THAT THEY WERE
BUZZARDS, BUT JOINED THEM ANYWAY. AS THEY
SOARED, SEVERAL OF THE BUZZARDS OBSERVED A
ROAD KILL AND, AS WAS THEIR NATURE, WENT TO
FEED. AS HE SOARED WITH THE REST OF THE FLOCK
HE WATCHED THOSE FEEDING AND GRADUALLY
ACCEPTED THIS NEW WAY OF FEEDING INTO HIS
SUBCONSCIOUS. A LITTLE LATER IN THE DAY HE
SPOTTED A NEW ROAD KILL AND DOVE TO CLAIM
IT. AS HE ATE, A VEHICLE CAME ALONG AND TOOK
HIS LIFE. HE HAD FORGOTTEN THAT HE WAS AN
EAGLE AND MENT TO LIVE LIKE ONE.
                          AUTHOR UNKNOWN

852. SANSKRIT PROVERB:
LOOK TO THIS DAY, FOR IT IS LIFE, THE VERY
LIFE OF LIFE. IN ITS BRIEF COURSE LIES ALL THE
REALITIES AND VERITIES OF EXISTENCE, THE BLISS
OF GROWTH, THE SPLENDOR OF ACTION, THE GLORY
OF POWER – FOR YESTERDAY IS BUT A DREAM AND
TOMORROW IS ONLY A VISION. BUT TODAY, WELL
LIVED, MAKES EVERY YESTERDAY A DREAM OF
HAPPINESS AND EVERY TOMORROW A VISION OF
HOPE. LOOK WELL, THEREFORE, TO THIS DAY.

853. SUCCESS:
TO LAUGH OFTEN AND MUCH; TO WIN RESPECT
OF INTELLIGENT PEOPLE AND THE AFFECTION OF
CHILDREN; TO EARN THE APPRECIATION OF HONEST
CRITICS AND ENDURE THE BETRAYAL OF FALSE
FRIENDS; TO APPRECIATE BEAUTY; TO FIND THE BEST
IN OTHERS; TO LEAVE THE WORLD A BIT BETTER,
WHETHER BY A HEALTHY CHILD, A GARDEN PATCH,
OR A REDEEMED SOCIAL CONDITION; TO KNOW EVEN
ONE LIFE HAS BEEN BREATHED EASIER BECAUSE YOU
LIVED. THIS IS TO HAVE SUCCEEDED.
                            HARRY EMERSON FOSDICK

854. IN RECOVERY WE TURN THE BLAME-THROWER OFF.

855. I ONLY NEED ABOUT 52 MEETINGS A YEAR TO
MAINTAIN MY RECOVERY, BUT I HAVE TO GO
TO 365 MEETINGS A YEAR TO MAKE SURE THAT
I GET TO THE ONES THAT I NEED.

856. CHECK YOURSELF, BEFORE YOU WREAK YOURSELF.

857. NO ONE EVER GRADUATES FROM RECOVERY,
BUT THERE ARE THOSE WHO DROP OUT.

858. REPETITION IS A VITAL KEY TO RECOVERY.

859. ROW, ROW, ROW YOUR BOAT (NOT MINE) GENTLY
DOWN (NOT UP) THE STREAM, AND MERRILY, MERRILY,
MERRILY, MERRILY, YOUR LIFE WILL BECOME A
DREAM (IN RECOVERY).

860. THE 12 STEPS OF RECOVERY ARE LIKE A
BULLETPROOF VEST, BUT YOU STILL HAVE TO
ACCEPT THE BRUISES AS YOU LIVE YOUR LIFE.

861. IN RECOVERY WE LEARN TO REPLACE COPPING
WITH COPING.

862. HAVING A RESENTMENT IS LIKE STABBING
YOURSELF AND EXPECTING SOMEONE ELSE
TO BLEED.

863. IDENTIFY YOUR WAY INTO RECOVERY OR
COMPARE YOUR WAY OUT TO YOUR ADDICTION.

864. WE REACH OUR BOTTOM WHEN WE STOP DIGGING.

865. IN RECOVERY, SOME THINGS ARE TAUGHT AND
SOME THINGS ARE CAUGHT.

866. WITHOUT ABSTINENCE I CAN'T GET RECOVERY
AND WITHOUT RECOVERY I CAN'T MAINTAIN
MY ABSTINENCE.

867. THE ONLY THING "NORMAL" IN LIFE IS THE CYCLE
ON A WASHING MACHINE.

868. MY UNCONTROLLABILITY OF MY CONTROL OVER MY
ADDICTION KEEPS ME IN MY RECOVERY.

869. WHEN YOU GET THE JOB, THE CAR, THE HOUSE,
THE BANK ACCOUNT, AND THE SIGNIFICANT
OTHER REMEMBER HOW YOU GOT THEM.

870. A MEETING A DAY KEEPS A RELAPSE AWAY.

871. BROKEN DREAMS:
AS CHILDREN BRING THEIR BROKEN TOYS
WITH TEARS FOR US TO MEND, I BROUGHT
MY BROKEN DREAMS TO GOD BECAUSE HE
WAS MY FRIEND. BUT INSTEAD OF LEAVING
HIM IN PEACE TO WORK ALONE, I HUNG AROUND
AND TRIED TO HELP WITH WAYS THAT WERE
OF MY OWN. AT LAST I SNATCHED THEM BACK
AND CRIED, "HOW CAN YOU BE SO SLOW?"
"MY CHILD." HE SAID, "WHAT COULD I DO?
YOU NEVER LET THEM GO!"
AUTHOR UNKNOWN

872. EACH ONE REACH ONE TO TEACH ONE TO REACH ONE.

873. RECOVERY LITERATURE: IF YOU DON'T PICK IT UP, IT WON'T GET IN YOU.

874. SOME OF US HAVE "TEA BAG" RECOVERY BECAUSE IT ONLY WORKS WHEN WE'RE IN HOT WATER.

875. B.I.B.L.E.: BASIC INSTRUCTIONS BEFORE LEAVING EARTH.

876. UNCOVER TO DISCOVER TO RECOVER IS THE FOURTH STEP SIMPLIFIED.

877. SOME OF US ARE SO GRATEFUL NOT TO HAVE DIARRHEA OF THE STOMACH THAT WE DEVELOP DIARRHEA OF THE MOUTH.

878. IN OUR SEARCH FOR THE ROSES IN LIFE WE SOMETIMES OVERLOOK THE BUTTERCUPS.

879. THE ROOM OF RECOVERY HAVE ENOUGH LOVERS AND SPEAKERS, BUT NOT ENOUGH SOLDIERS.

880. WE MAY NOT HAVE IT ALL TOGETHER, BUT TOGETHER WE HAVE IT ALL.

881. IF NOTHING CHANGES, YOUR CLEAN DATE WILL.

882. IT WORKS IF YOU WORK IT AND IT WORKS IF YOU DON'T.

883. IF YOU DON'T WORK IT, IT WORKS YOU.

884. HOME GROUP COFFEE: THE FIRST CUP IS OUR FAULT AND THE SECOND CUP IS YOUR FAULT.

885. SHOW ME YOUR FRIENDS AND I'LL SHOW YOU WHO YOU ARE.

886. ANYTHING THAT YOU CAN CRITICIZE, YOU CAN BECOME.

887. WHEN YOU'RE GREEN YOU GROW AND WHEN YOU'RE RIPE YOU ROT.

888. FAITH WITHOUT WORKS IS FEAR.

889. THE ROOMS OF RECOVERY ARE PLACES WHERE MISFITS FIT.

890. THE ROOMS OF RECOVERY MAY BE DIFFERENT, BUT THE PROGRAM OF RECOVERY WILL ALWAYS BE THE SAME.

891. BEFORE I CAME INTO RECOVERY, I WAS CRUCIFYING MYSELF WITH RESENTMENTS.

892. FEAR IS THE PATHWAY TO RELAPSE.

893. FEAR IS A FEELING AND FEELINGS CANNOT KILL YOU.

894. LET ME ALWAYS LOVE THE BEST IN OTHERS AND NEVER FEAR THEIR WORST.

895. PAIN IS THE TOUCHSTONE OF PROGRESS.

896. THIS EXPERIENCE CAN BE TURNED INTO A BENEFIT.

897. THE DAY THAT I REALIZED THAT I COULD NOT THROW MY LIFE AWAY, BECAUSE OF IT WAS DAMAGED A LITTLE, I ENTERED INTO MY RECOVERY.

898. IF I DO NOT CHANGE THE WAY THAT I THINK AND ACT, MY FEELINGS WILL NOT CHANGE EITHER.

899. LETTING GO:
TO LET GO DOES NOT MEAN TO STOP CARING, IT
  MEANS I CAN NOT DO IT FOR SOMEONE ELSE.
TO LET GO IS NOT TO CUT MYSELF OFF, IT IS THE
  REALIZATION THAT I CAN NOT CONTROL ANOTHER.
TO LET GO IS NOT TO ENABLE, BUT TO ALLOW
  LEARNING FROM NATURAL CONSEQUENCES.
TO LET GO IS TO ADMIT POWERLESSNESS, WHICH

MEANS THE OUTCOME IS NOT IN MY HANDS.
TO LET GO IS NOT TO TRY TO CHANGE OR BLAME
ANOTHER, I CAN ONLY CHANGE MYSELF.
TO LET GO IS NOT TO CARE FOR, BUT TO CARE ABOUT.
TO LET GO IS NOT TO FIX, BUT TO BE SUPPORTIVE.
TO LET GO IS NOT TO JUDGE, BUT TO ALLOW ANOTHER
TO BE A HUMAN BEING.
TO LET GO IS NOT TO BE IN THE MIDDLE, ARRANGING
ALL THE OUTCOMES, BUT TO ALLOW OTHERS TO
EFFECT THEIR OWN OUTCOMES.
TO LET GO IS NOT TO BE PROTECTIVE, IT IS TO PERMIT
ANOTHER TO FACE REALITY.
TO LET GO IS NOT TO DENY, BUT TO ACCEPT.
TO LET GO IS NOT TO NAG, SCOLD, OR ARGUE, BUT TO
SEARCH OUT MY OWN SHORTCOMINGS AND TO
CORRECT THEM.
TO LET GO IS NOT TO ADJUST EVERYTHING TO MY
DESIRES, BUT TO TAKE EACH DAY AS IT COMES AND
TO CHERISH THE MOMENTS.
TO LET GO IS NOT TO CRITICIZE AND REGULATE
ANYONE, BUT TO TRY TO BECOME WHAT DREAM I
CAN BE.
TO LET GO IS NOT TO REGRET THE PAST, BUT TO GROW
AND LIVE THE FUTURE.
TO LET GO IS TO FEAR LESS AND TO LOVE MORE.
AUTHOR UNKNOWN

900. IF I DO NOT WANT TO DO SOMETHING TO HELP ME
IN MY RECOVERY, THEN I HAVE TO DO THAT SAME
SOMETHING TWICE: ONCE FOR MY RECOVERY AND
ONCE FOR REPETITION.

901. LOVE OF A MAID, LOVE OF A MOTHER, THERE
IS NO GREATER LOVE THAN ONE DRUNK FOR
ANOTHER.

902. SPIRITUAL RECOVERY IS A LONG ROAD, BUT ONE
STEP AT A TIME WILL GET ME THERE.

903. IF I DON'T:
GET TO MEETINGS,
GET A HOME GROUP,
GET INVOLVED IN "MY" RECOVERY,
GET A SPONSOR,
GET TO CHANGING PEOPLE, PLACES, AND THINGS,

GET TO PRAYING,
GET A COMMITMENT,
GET TO "STEPPING."
GET TO APPLYING THE STEPS INTO "MY" LIFE,
GET TO CARRYING THE MESSAGE OF RECOVERY, AND
GET TO SPONSORING PEOPLE,
THEN I WILL GET TO LIVING IN MY DISEASE AGAIN.
                                    GEORGE M.   2004

904. MY ONLY LIMITATIONS ARE THOSE THAT I IMPOSE
     UPON MYSELF.

905. THE MEASURE OF RECOVERY, WITH ALL OF ITS MANY
     FACTORS, CAN NEVER BE DISTORTED BECAUSE I HAVE
     A DEVINE RESPONSIBILITY TO HELP OTHERS FIND OUT
     ABOUT US WITH EASE.

906. WHEN MY DISEASE CONFRONTS ME ABOUT MY PAST, I
     ASK MY DISEASE ABOUT ITS FUTURE.

907. I AM 99% SURE THAT I AM NOT ALWAYS 100% RIGHT.

908. MY DISEASE DEFINED: MY STINKING THINKING.

909. AS A CHILD I WALKED ON PEOPLES TOES AND
     AS AN ADULT, CAUGHT UP IN MY DISEASE, I
     WALKED ON PEOPLES HEARTS.

910. I USE TO CRY, "CLEAN" TO REST IN MY ADDICTION,
     BUT I REALLY NEEDED TO CRY TO MY HIGHER POWER
     TO ARREST MY ADDICTION.

911. WORK THE PROGRAM OF RECOVERY AND
     NOT YOUR NETWORK OR YOUR SPONSOR.

912. I HAD TO GET INVOLVED IN MY RECOVERY
     OR I WOULD GET INVOLVED IN MY DISEASE.

913. GETTING DRUNK IS THE SIDE EFFECT OF DRINKING.

914. GIVE TO MAN THAT WHICH YOU ARE RESPONSIBLE
     AND GIVE TO YOUR HIGHER POWER THAT WHICH IS
     ASKED.

915. WHEN I USED AND ABUSED DRUGS, (ALCOHOL IS A
DRUG – AMERICAN MEDICAL ASSOCIATION, 1956) I
USED AND ABUSED THOSE WHO LOVED ME.

916. A MAN WITH NO MERCY IN HIS HEART LIVES IN A
PLACE WORSE THAN DEATH.

917. NEVER PUT PERSONALITIES BEFORE PRINCIPLES
BECAUSE SOONER OR LATER YOU WILL LOSE.

918. SPIRITUAL GROWTH:
"THERE IS A PRINCIPLE WHICH IS A BAR AGAINST ALL
INFORMATION, WHICH IS PROOF AGAINST ALL
ARGUMENTS, AND WHICH CANNOT FAIL TO KEEP A
MAN IN EVERLASTING IGNORANCE – THAT PRINCIPLE
IS CONTEMPT PRIOR TO INVESTIGATION."
HERBERT SPENCER

919. SELF-PRAISE STINKS.

920. PREPARE AND EXECUTE.

921. I FEEL THE WAY THAT I FEEL BECAUSE I THINK
THE WAY THAT I THINK.

922. I CANNOT ALWAYS SAVE MY FACE AND MY ASS AT THE
SAME TIME IN RECOVERY.

923. IF I PRAY AND DO NOT DO THE WORK, IT IS A DEAD
PRAYER.

924. PART OF MY RECOVERY IS SITTING BACK AND
WATCHING THE SHOW.

925. I HAVE NEVER BEEN IN THE WRONG PLACE AT THE
WRONG TIME BECAUSE ABSOLUTELY NOTHING
HAPPENS IN GOD'S WORLD BY MISTAKE.

926. WITH ADDICTION CONSTANTLY GAZING UPON US, WE ALL
COULD SEE THAT OUR PAST ACTIONS BROUGHT ABOUT THE
END OF OUR DREAMS. ALL OF OUR PLANS AND ALL OF OUR I-
COULD-HAVE-BEENS HAD RUN OUT OF TIME. WE WERE ALONE
WITH PRECISELY WHAT WE HAVE BECOME. NO MORE AND NO
LESS. WE WERE ALONE AND LIVING WITHIN OURSELVES. THE
DENIAL HAD ENDED. WE HAD BECOME HUMBLE AND

DEMANDED HELP OR WE WOULD HAVE DIED. THANK
GOD THAT THERE WERE THOSE WHO HAD BEEN WHERE WE
WERE AND STRETCHED OUT THEIR HAND TO US OR GAVE US A
CARING HUG. THANK GOD FOR THE ROOMS AND THE STEPS
OF RECOVERY.   THANK GOD ... PERIOD.

927. ALL SPIRITUAL EVOLUTION IS SELF-EVOLUTION. IT
      BEGINS WITH THE ACCEPTANCE OF ALL THAT WAS,
      ALL THAT IS, AND ALL THAT WILL BE. IT IS NURTURED
      WHEN I PASS ON TO ANOTHER HUMAN BEING THAT
      WHICH MY HIGHER POWER REVEALS TO ME.
                                        GEORGE M. 2004

928. I DID NOT RELAPSE! I TOOK A "LEAVE OF ABSTINENCE."

929. I CANNOT ARTICULATE MY RECOVERY; I HAVE TO
      DEMONSTRATE MY RECOVERY.

930. DEPRESSION DEFINED: ANGER TURNED INWARD.

931. WHEN I WAS YOUNG MY PARENTS WOULD TELL ME,
      "IF YOU STAY ON THE STEPS YOU WON'T GET INTO
      ANY SERIOUS TROUBLE." AND WHEN I CAME INTO
      RECOVERY I HEARD, "IF YOU STAY ON THE STEPS YOU
      WON'T GET INTO ANY SERIOUS TROUBLE."

932. MY EYES ARE THE WINDOW OF MY SOUL AND EVERY
      ONCE IN A WHILE THEY NEED A GOOD WASHING (CRY)
      SO THAT I CAN SEE MORE CLEARLY THROUGH THEM.

933. CHARACTER DEFINED: THE MORAL OR ETHICAL
      STRUCTURE OF A PERSON.

934. DEFECT DEFINED: THE LACK OF SOMETHING
      NECESSARY OR DESIRABLE.

935. SHORTCOMING DEFINED: LACKING AN ESSENTIAL
      ELEMENT OR PART; INCOMPLETE.

936. THE "FOUR HORSEMEN": TERROR, BEWILDERMENT,
      FRUSTRATION, AND DESPAIR.
                 ALCOHOLICS ANONYMOUS, THIRD EDITION, PAGE 151

937. CHANGE YOUR THOUGHTS AND CHANGE YOUR
      WORLD.

938. PEOPLE WHO DO NOT HAVE A DRINKING PROBLEM DO NOT THINK ABOUT THEIR DRINKING.

939. I CAME FOR MY DRINKING AND I STAYED FOR MY THINKING.

940. COMING INTO RECOVERY AND NOT WANTING TO CHANGE IS LIKE TAKING A LAXATIVE AND NOT WANTING TO SHIT.

941. EVEN AFTER YEARS OF RECOVERY I STILL HAVE TO STAY AWAY FROM SLIPPERY PEOPLE WHO GO TO SLIPPERY PLACES AND DO SLIPPERY THINGS.

942. COMMITMENTS IN RECOVERY WILL NOT CHANGE THE WAY I THINK AND THAT IS WHY I APPLY THE STEPS INTO MY LIFE.

943. AS LONG AS I STAY IN RECOVERY EVERY DAY IS A HOLIDAY.

944. GOD'S WILL FOR ME IS A SURPRISE.

945. THE TWELVE STEPS SHOWED ME WHO I WAS BY BEING WILLING, HONEST, AND OPEN-MINDED.

946. THINK RECOVERY AND RECOVERY WILL THINK FOR YOU.

947. TOUGH GUYS CANNOT TOTALLY ENJOY A SIMPLE ROLLER-COASTER RIDE.

948. THERE ARE A LOT OF PEOPLE IN THE ROOMS OF RECOVERY, BUT THERE IS NOT A LOT OF RECOVERY IN SOME OF THE PEOPLE IN THE ROOMS.

949. THE SHORTEST DISTANCE BETWEEN TWO POINTS IS A STRAIGHT LINE:
ADDICTION => 1, 2, 3, 4, 5, 6, 7, 8, 9, 10, 11, 12 => SERENITY.

950. IN RECOVERY WE DO NOT READ BETWEEN THE LINES OF THE "BASIC TEXT."

951. I STAY IN RECOVERY BECAUSE MY REHAB DID NOT GIVE ME A "DO-IT-AGAIN" CARD.

952. I DID NOT GIVE IN TO RECOVERY, I CAVED INTO RECOVERY.

953. BEFORE I CAME INTO RECOVERY I USE TO BE A PROFESSIONAL VOLUNTEER FOR A SUBJECTIVE, PERSONALIZED STUDY CONCERNING VARIOUS ADDICTIONS.

954. YOU CANNOT STUMBLE IF YOU ARE ON YOUR KNEES.

955. IN RECOVERY WHAT WE CANNOT LOVE UNCONDITIONALLY WE CAN LEARN TO TOLERATE.

956. ATTITUDE:
"THE LONGER I LIVE, THE MORE I REALIZE THE IMPACT OF ATTITUDE ON LIFE. ATTITUDE, TO ME, IS MORE IMPORTANT THAN FACTS. IT IS MORE IMPORTANT THAN THE PAST, THAN EDUCATION, THAN MONEY, THAN CIRCUMSTANCES, THAN FAILURES, THAN SUCCESSES, THAN WHAT OTHER PEOPLE THINK OR SAY OR DO. IT IS MORE IMPORTANT THAN APPEARANCE, GIFTEDNESS, OR SKILL. IT WILL MAKE OR BREAK A COMPANY ... A CHURCH ... A HOME. THE REMARKABLE THING IS WE HAVE A CHOICE EVERY DAY REGARDING THE ATTITUDE WE WILL EMBRACE FOR THAT DAY. WE CANNOT CHANGE OUR PAST ... WE CANNOT CHANGE THE FACT THAT PEOPLE WILL ACT IN A CERTAIN WAY. WE CANNOT CHANGE THE INEVITABLE. THE ONLY THING WE CAN DO IS PLAY ON THE ONE STRING WE HAVE, AND THAT IS OUR ATTITUDE. I AM CONVINCED THAT LIFE IS 10% WHAT HAPPENS TO ME AND 90%   HOW I REACT TO IT. AND SO IT IS WITH YOU ... WE ARE IN CHARGE OF OUR ATTITUDES."
                                        CHARLES SWINDALL

957. PEACE IS NOT THE ABSENCE OF TROUBLE, PEACE IS THE AWARENESS OF GOD'S PRESENCE.

958. THE TEST IS NOT IN THE STRENGTH OF THE STORM; THE TEST IS IN THE FIRMNESS OF THE FOUNDATION.

959. WHEN I STARTED TO CHANGE MY PLAY MATES, PLAY THINGS, AND PLAY GROUNDS, I STARTED TO CHANGE.

960. IF I AM NOT WORKING ON MY RECOVERY, I AM WORKING ON MY RELAPSE.

961. MY "RELAPSE RECORD" WENT 1, 2, 3, SKIP ... 1, 2, 3, SKIP ... 1, 2, 3, SKIP ON 78 R.P.M.'S.

962. A "D.W.W." (DRINKING WHILE WALKING) LEAD ME TO THE ROOMS OF RECOVERY.

963. IF I DO NOT DO THIS RECOVERY THING ONE DAY AT A TIME, I WILL NOT GET ANY TIME IN RECOVERY.

964. THE TWELVE STEPS GAVE ME A HIGHER POWERED EDUCATION.

965. THE FRONT ROW AT EVERY MEETING IS THE "CRITICAL CARE" ROW.

966. FEAR IS THE FEELING THAT WILL SLOW DOWN MY SPIRITUAL RECOVERY.

967. IF I EVER THINK THAT "I HAVE GOT THIS THING," I WILL PROBABLY SLACK UP ON MY MEETINGS, WHICH WILL BRING ABOUT MY DIS-EASE AND OPEN THE DOOR TO MY DISEASE.

968. RELATIONSHIPS CAN BRUISE ME EMOTIONALLY AND SPIRITUALLY, BUT THEY CANNOT KILL ME.

969. A REBELLIOUS REFUSAL TO WORK ON MY GLARING COLLECTION OF CHARACTER DEFECTS IS DESTRUCTIVE TO MY RECOVERY.

970. FREEDOM FROM MY ADDICTION AND ALL OF ITS CONSEQUENCES CAN ONLY BE ACHIEVED BY BELIEVING AND TRUSTING IN MY HIGHER POWER'S WILL FOR ME.

971 ALL OF THE PROGRESS IN RECOVERY CAN BE REDUCED TO TWO SIMPLE WORDS: HUMILITY AND RESPONSIBILITY.

972. A DRUNKEN MAN WILL DO WHAT A SOBER MAN THINKS.

973. I USE TO ABUSE MYSELF MENTALLY, PHYSICALLY, AND SPIRITUALLY ONE DAY AT A TIME, BUT NOW I HAVE LEARNED TO RECOVER ONE DAY AT A TIME.

974. ALTHOUGH I CARRY THE MESSAGE ON 12TH STEP CALLS, I CANNOT TAKE CREDIT FOR ANY ONES RECOVERY OR THEIR RELAPSE.

975. IN RECOVERY, NOBODY CAN MAKE YOU BEHAVE OR PUNISH YOU IF YOU DO NOT. THAT IS WHAT OUR TWELVE STEPS AND TWELVE TRADITIONS ARE ABOUT: SPIRITUAL GROWTH AND FREEDOM.

976. THE COMPULSION AMONG SOME OF US IN RECOVERY TO SURVIVE AND TO GROW SOON BECOMES FAR STRONGER THAN THE TEMPTATION TO RESUME OUR DESTRUCTION OR TO MISBEHAVE.

977. I MUST INCREASE THE PRACTICE OF OUR SPIRITUAL PRINCIPLES OUT OF A DEEP RESPECT AND SENSE OF RESPONSIBILITY TO MY RECOVERY.

978. WHEN MY WILLINGNESS, HONESTY, OPEN-MINDEDNESS, AND ACCEPTANCE BECAME ONE WITHIN ME, I FOUND THAT ALL OF MY REBELLION TOWARDS OUR SPIRITUAL PRINCIPLES DISAPPEAR.

979. IF A DUCK HAS "LIPS" THEN I HAVE AN ADDICTION.

980. WE ALL GET TO THE ROOMS OF RECOVERY WHEN IT IS OUR TIME TO.

981. JUST FOR TODAY I AM LIVING AND MENDING FRACTURES WITHIN MY LIFE.

982. EASY DOES NOT DO SHIT AND NEITHER DOES PROCRASTINATION: IT TAKES TIME AND EFFORT!

983. I DO NOT BELIEVE IN MIRACLES ... I RELY ON THEM.

984. "JUST FOR TODAY" IS A SPIRITUAL THING.

985. IF YOU ARE GOING TO WORRY, DO NOT PRAY AND IF YOU ARE GOING TO PRAY, DO NOT WORRY.

986. SOME OF US SAW OUR BOTTOM AND STOPPED, WHILE OTHERS OF US HAD TO HIT OUR BOTTOM IN ORDER TO STOP.

987. SAVE THE DRAMA FOR YOUR MOMMA.

988. I USE TO BE THE SMARTEST PERSON I EVER INTRODUCED MYSELF TO.

989. PRAYER CHANGES THINGS.

990. IN RECOVERY WE WILL ALLOW YOU TO BE WHOEVER YOU THINK THAT YOU ARE.

991. THE TWELVE STEPS PLACED ME ON THE PATH OF RECOVERY AND THEN MY HIGHER POWER PLACED ME ON THE PATH OF A RICH AND REWARDING LIFE.

992. DURING MY ADDICTION I BECAME WILLING TO GO TO ANY LENGTH AND NOW I MAINTAIN THIS SAME ATTITUDE TOWARDS MY RECOVERY.

993. IN THE ROOMS OF RECOVERY I LISTEN FOR THE LANGUAGE OF THE HEART TO AID ME IN MY RECOVERY.

994. I USE TO RELY ON THE SYMPATHY OF OTHERS TO FEED MY ADDICTION, NOW I RELY OF THE EMPATHY OF OTHERS TO FEED MY RECOVERY.

995. A PERSON DOES NOT HAVE TO BE IN THE ROOMS OF RECOVERY FOR MY HIGHER POWER TO SPEAK TO ME.

996. I AM WORKING "MY" PROGRAM AND NOT "THE" PROGRAM OF RECOVERY BY READING BETWEEN THE LINES OF THE "BASIC TEXT."

997. THE IMAGE I USE TO PORTRAY TO THOSE AROUND ME WAS, IN REALITY, THAT OF A ROUGH, TOUGH CREAM PUFF.

998. "WORK" IN THE ROOMS OF RECOVERY DEFINED: APPLYING THE STEPS OF RECOVERY INTO DAILY LIFE.

999. THE THERAPEUTIC VALUE OF ONE RECOVERING PERSON HELPING ANOTHER, WITHOUT EXCEPTIONS OR EXPECTATIONS, IS WITHOUT PARALLEL.

1000. I CANNOT MEASURE THE UNCONDITIONAL LOVE I HAVE FOR OTHERS, BOTH INSIDE AND OUTSIDE THE ROOMS OF RECOVERY, BY LOOKING AT THE THINGS THAT I SAY AND DO, BUT I CAN MEASURE THAT LOVE BY LETTING OTHERS BE EXACTLY WHERE THEY WANT TO BE.

1001. THE TWELVE SPIRITURAL PRINCIPLES OF RECOVERY:
HONESTY
HOPE
FAITH
COURAGE
INTEGRITY
WILLINGNESS
HUMILITY
LOVE
SELF-DISCIPLINE
PERSERVERANCE
AWARENESS
SERVICE.

MORE WILL BE REVEALED . . . .

MY THOUGHTS, SLOGANS, AND STORIES

* H.O.P.E.S. = Honest, Open, People Enjoying Sobriety.

* All of my nevers are floating on the Sea of Not Yet and if I decide to take
  a dip I just may have to hold onto one of them to survive my addiction.

MY THOUGHTS, SLOGANS, AND STORIES

MY THOUGHTS, SLOGANS, AND STORIES

MY THOUGHTS, SLOGANS, AND STORIES

MY THOUGHTS, SLOGANS, AND STORIES

MY THOUGHTS, SLOGANS, AND STORIES

MY THOUGHTS, SLOGANS, AND STORIES

www.ingramcontent.com/pod-product-compliance
Lightning Source LLC
Chambersburg PA
CBHW071017040426
42443CB00007B/818